MY FIRST ENCYCLOPEDIA

My First Encyclopedia

This is a Parragon Publishing Book
This edition published in 2004

Parragon Publishing
Queen Street House
4 Queen Street
Bath BA1 1HE, UK

Copyright © Parragon 2003

This edition was created by
Starry Dog Books

Consultant Editor
Brian Williams

Author and Editor
Neil Morris

British Library Cataloguing-in-Publication Data

A catalogue record for this book is
available from the British Library

ISBN 1-40541-706-4

Printed in India

Contents

Introduction

An encyclopedia is a book that contains all kinds of information. In this children's encyclopedia, the information is presented in six sections: Earth and Space, Science, Human Body, Animals, Long Long Ago, and People and Places. Each of these sections gives a wide coverage of the subject matter, offering information through nineteen topics.

All the information in this book is presented in an interesting, highly visual way. There are hundreds of photographs, illustrations, and even cartoons, all with explanatory text.

A comprehensive index is there to help readers find the information they are looking for. There is also a helpful page of New Words, where difficult words or technical terms are explained.

In addition, a fun quiz appears at the end of each section. All the quiz questions are answered in the book, and the particular page giving the information is listed after each question.

To add to the interest, each section has simple projects. In each case, the clear photograph shows the end result that is possible and acts as an encouragement to attempt the project. Some are fun craft ideas, while others are easy experiments. Above all, this book is meant to interest, entertain, and amuse children. It is intended to be fun to use and dip into, so that children will come back to it... again and again.

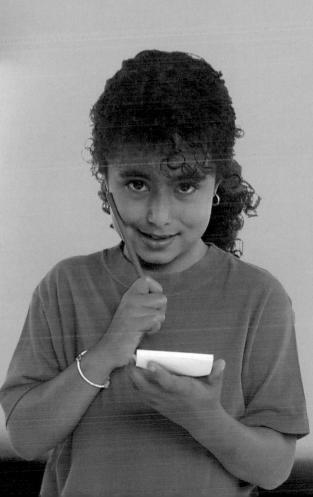

How to use this book

In this book, every page is filled with information on the sort of topics that you will enjoy reading about.
Information is given in photographs and illustrations, as well as in words. All the pictures are explained by captions, to tell you what you are looking at and to give even more detailed facts.

THE CARTOONS throughout the book are not meant to be taken too seriously! Hopefully the pictures will make you laugh, but the text that goes with them gives real information.

MAIN TEXT introduces each topic. Every time you turn the page, you will find a new topic.

CAPTIONS give interesting information about the pictures. An arrow at the start of each caption points to the right picture.

BEAUTIFUL PHOTOGRAPHS have been specially chosen to bring each subject to life.

Earth and Space

Mountains

There are high mountains all over the world. They took millions of years to form, as the plates that make up the Earth's crust pressed together and buckled.

Mountain ranges that lie near the edge of plates are still being pushed higher. They have steep, rocky peaks. Older ranges that lie farther from the plate edges have been worn away over the years by rain, wind, and ice.

The longest and highest mountain ranges, such as the Andes of South America and the Himalayas to the north of India, form huge mountain systems. Few animals or people live on the highest mountains. The ten highest mountains on land are all in the Himalayas. The highest peak of all, Mount Everest, lies on the border between Nepal and Tibet. It is 29,028 feet (8,848 m) high and is known to the people of Tibet as Chomolongma, or "goddess mother of the

WHAT IS AN IBEX?
The ibex is a wild mountain goat that lives in the high mountains in some parts of the world. Ibexes are sure-footed and happy to climb along rocky crags. Male ibexes have long horns, which they sometimes use to fight each other.

✪ **Block mountains** *are created when the Earth's crust develops cracks, called faults, and the chunk of land between them is pushed up.*

36

✪ **The Earth's plates** *are made up of layers of rock, called strata. As the plates move, the strata are bent into folds. On mountain rock-faces, you can often see how the layers have been folded into wavy lines.*

MOUNTAINS OF JUNK
PROJECT Crumple newspaper into big balls and tape them onto a cardboard base. Make papier-mâché pulp by soaking newspaper pieces in a bucket of wallpaper paste. Cover the balls with the pulp to make mountains and valleys. When your landscape is dry, paint some snow-capped peaks with white paint. Sprinkle the base with sand. You could add a mountain lake.

✪ **The longest mountain range** *on land is the Andes, which stretches for over 4,000 miles (7,000 km) along the west coast of South America. The Transantarctic Mountains stretch right across the frozen continent of Antarctica.*

✪ **Dome mountains** *form when the top layers of the Earth's crust are pushed up by molten rock underneath. This makes a big bulge.*

✪ **Fold mountains** *are formed when one plate bumps and pushes against another. Rock is squeezed up into folds. The Andes were made this way.*

Earth and Space

37

ILLUSTRATIONS are clear and simple, and sometimes they are cut away so that you can see inside things.

PROJECT BOXES describe craft activities related to the topic. These are things to make or simple experiments to do. The photograph helps to show you what to do, and is there to inspire you to have a try! But remember, some of the activities can be quite messy, so put old newspaper down first. Always use round-ended scissors, and ask an adult for help if you are unsure of something or need sharp tools or materials.

Earth and Space

Our home, Earth, is just one of the nine planets that travel around our star, the Sun. And the Sun is really just an ordinary star, like many millions of others in the Universe. Scientists already know an enormous amount about the Universe and space, and yet there is still much more to learn in the future.

On Earth, there are interesting things to see and learn about, from rocky mountains to deep oceans, and from thick forests to sandy deserts. Some of the things we humans do every day are threatening to spoil our planet, but we can all help to make the world a better place.

Our Planet

We live on the planet Earth. On our planet there are high mountains and hot deserts, huge oceans and freezing cold regions.

A blanket of air is wrapped around the Earth. This air allows us to breathe and live. Beyond the air, our planet is surrounded by space. A long way away in space, there are other planets and stars. Most planets have satellites, or moons, which circle around them. Our Moon is about 240,000 miles (385,000 km) away from Earth.

◁ **From space,** *Earth looks like a mainly blue and white planet. It looks blue because water covers most of its surface. The white swirling patterns are clouds, and the brown and green areas are land. Earth has a diameter of about 7,900 miles (12,700 km), almost four times bigger than the Moon.*

◆ **The Moon** circles the Earth once a month. On its journey, different amounts of its sunlit side can be seen from Earth. This makes the Moon seem to change shape during the month.

The Moon spins as it circles the Earth, so the same side always faces us. People had never seen the other side of the Moon until a spacecraft traveled around it.

▶ **The Moon's surface** is pitted with craters. These holes were made by chunks of space rock crashing into the Moon. Early scientists called the flat areas "seas," but there is no water, or air, on the Moon.

◀ **The Moon** was probably formed when a huge asteroid crashed into the Earth billions of years ago. The crash threw rock fragments into space, and these came together to form the Moon.

The Solar System

Nine planets, including Earth, travel around the Sun. Along with moons, comets, and lumps of rock, they make up the Solar System.

This system is Earth's local neighborhood in space. Everything in it is connected to the Sun by a force that we cannot see. This force is called gravity.

The largest planet, Jupiter, is big enough to hold over 1,300 Earths. The smallest planet, Pluto, is smaller even than our Moon.

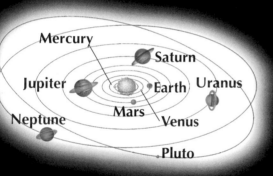

◀ **The planets** *have different orbits around the Sun. In a gap between Mars and Jupiter, there are thousands of miniature planets, called asteroids. Pluto is usually the farthest planet from the Sun, but sometimes its path crosses Neptune's. Mercury is a small, rocky planet. It is closest to the Sun and travels around it six times in one of our Earth years.*

▶ **Among the planets** *there are four giants—Jupiter, Saturn, Uranus, and Neptune. Each has a small rocky core, surrounded by a thick layer of ice or liquid, with gas on the outside. Along with Pluto, these giants are called the outer planets.*

Mercury

Venus

Earth

Mars

PLANETS NAMED AFTER ROMAN GODS

MERCURY, messenger of the gods

VENUS, goddess of love

MARS, god of war

JUPITER, king of the gods

SATURN, father of Jupiter

URANUS, god of the heavens

NEPTUNE, god of the sea

PLUTO, god of the Underworld

Uranus

Pluto

Neptune

Saturn

Jupiter

MODEL PLANETS

PROJECT

Mold modeling clay around beads, marbles, and ping-pong balls to make planets. Earth can be blue and white, Mars red, and Jupiter orange. Mold a big yellow Sun around a tennis ball. Use black cardboard for a space background and arrange the nine planets in the right order. You could label each one.

Our Star

Our Solar System has one star, which we call the Sun. The sunlight that gives us life is the light of our burning star.

The Sun is a vast, fiery ball of gases. The hottest part of the Sun is its core, where energy is produced. The Sun burns steadily and its energy provides the Earth with heat and light. We could not live without the Sun's light, which takes just over eight minutes to travel through space and reach us. You must never look directly at the Sun. Its light is too strong and would harm your eyes.

prominence

◐ **Stars cluster together** *in groups called galaxies. The Sun is just one of billions of stars in our galaxy, which is called the Milky Way. It got its name because, from Earth, it looks like a creamy band of stars across the sky.*

◑ **Stars seem to form patterns,** *known as constellations, in the night sky. The "signs of the zodiac" star-groups are used in horoscopes, but scientists do not believe the stars have anything to do with people's characters or futures.*

| Aquarius, the Water-carrier, Jan 20-Feb 18 | Pisces, the Fish, Feb 19-Mar 20 | Aries, the Ram, Mar 21-Apr 19 | Taurus, the Bull, Apr 20-May 20 | Gemini, the Twins, May 21-June 21 | Cancer, the Crab, June 22-July 22 | Leo, the Lion, July 23-Aug 22 | Virgo, the Virgin, Aug 23-Sept 22 |

core

sunspot

photosphere (Sun's surface)

radiative zone

convective zone

● **Heat from the core** *surges up to the Sun's surface, called the photosphere. Sunspots are dark, cooler patches. Prominences are jets of gas that erupt from the surface.*

Libra, the Scales, Sept 23- Oct 23

Scorpio, the Scorpion, Oct 24- Nov 21

Sagittarius, the Archer, Nov 22- Dec 21

Capricorn, the Goat, Dec 22- Jan 19

TWINKLE, TWINKLE, LITTLE STAR

Seen from Earth, stars seem to twinkle. This is because starlight passes through bands of hot and cold air around the Earth, and this makes the light flicker. In space, stars shine steadily.

The Universe

Our address in space is "Earth, Solar System, Milky Way Galaxy, Universe." The Universe is the biggest known thing there is and includes all the empty parts of space between the stars.

Most scientists think that the Universe began with a Big Bang, which happened billions of years ago. Since then it has been growing bigger and bigger in all directions, creating more and more space.

galaxies form

⊘ **Scientists believe** *that millions of years after the Big Bang, gases clustered into clouds. These clouds clumped together to form galaxies. The planets formed later from clouds of gas, dust, and rocks. As the Universe expands, the galaxies move farther apart.*

◐ **There are countless** *billions of stars in the Universe. Sometimes a very old star explodes. We call this a supernova. New stars are being created all the time in different sizes.*

clouds of gas

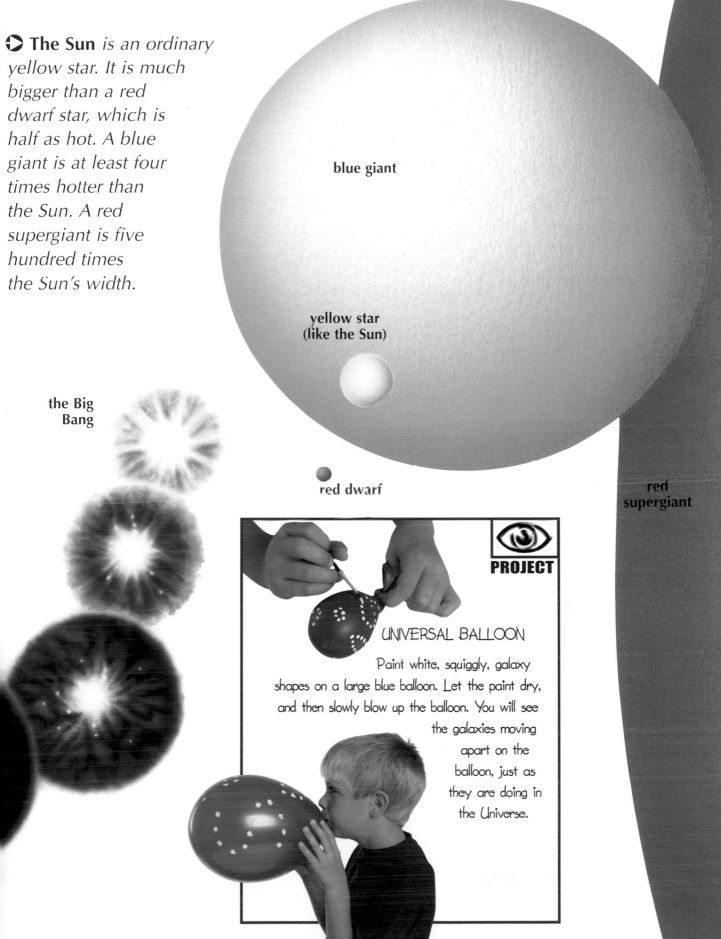

◐ **The Sun** is an ordinary yellow star. It is much bigger than a red dwarf star, which is half as hot. A blue giant is at least four times hotter than the Sun. A red supergiant is five hundred times the Sun's width.

blue giant

yellow star
(like the Sun)

the Big Bang

red dwarf

red supergiant

PROJECT

UNIVERSAL BALLOON

Paint white, squiggly, galaxy shapes on a large blue balloon. Let the paint dry, and then slowly blow up the balloon. You will see the galaxies moving apart on the balloon, just as they are doing in the Universe.

17

Days and Seasons

It takes a year for the Earth to travel all the way around the Sun. During that time the Earth spins around 365 times, giving that number of days. At the same time the Moon travels around the Earth 12 times, giving that number of months.

As the Earth travels around the Sun, it spins like a top. It turns right around once every 24 hours, and this gives us day and night. The part of the Earth facing the Sun is in daylight. When that part turns away from the Sun, it gets dark and has nighttime.

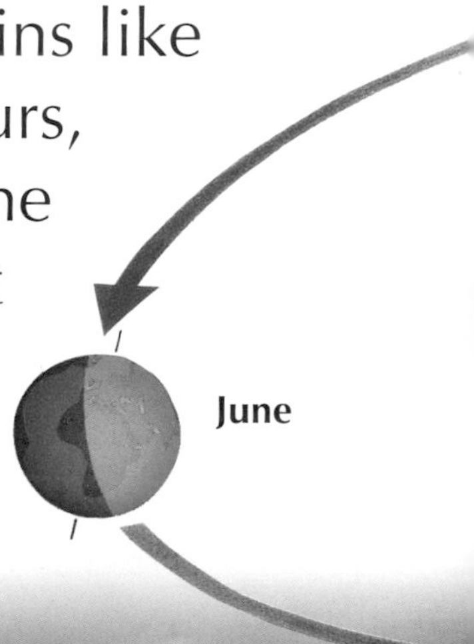

We have seasons because the Earth has a tilt. When the northern half of the Earth is tilted toward the Sun, it is summer there. At that time it is winter in the southern half of the world, because it is tilted away from the Sun's warmth.

June

spring

summer

❂ **In June** *the northern part of the Earth is tilted toward the Sun. It is summer there then, with long, light days and short, dark nights. In December it is the exact opposite. Then the Sun shines more directly on the southern part of the Earth and makes it warmer.*

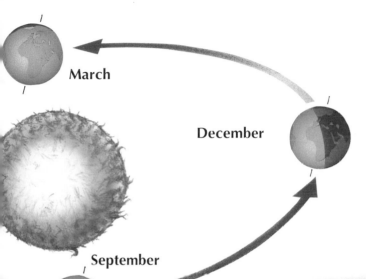

March

December

September

NIGHT AND DAY

PROJECT

In a darkened room, shine a flashlight at a globe of the Earth. If you don't have a globe, use a large ball. The globe or ball is the Earth, and your flashlight acts like the Sun as it shines on our planet. The side facing the Sun gets light, so there it is day. On the dark side of the globe it is night. You could slowly spin the Earth around, to see how day and night follow each other around the globe.

❂ **The Earth's landscape** *changes with the seasons. Many trees grow new leaves in spring. The leaves are green and fully grown in summer. They turn brown and start to drop in the fall. In winter, the trees' branches are bare. In some places around the middle of the Earth, near the equator, there are only two seasons. One part of the year is hot and dry, and the other part is warm and wet.*

fall

winter

Looking at the Sky

Since ancient times, people have learned a lot about the Universe by studying the night sky.

Early astronomers simply used their naked eyes. Modern astronomers look through big, powerful telescopes so that they can see planets and stars close up. Today, there is even a telescope out in space that sends pictures back to Earth.

◗ **This star map** *shows the star-groups you can see in a year if you live in the northern half of the world. The stars have been connected together to make constellation patterns. People who live in the southern half of the Earth see different patterns.*

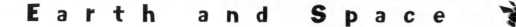

▶ **Big telescopes** *are usually housed in observatories. These are dome-shaped buildings, with a roof that can slide open to show part of the sky. The best observatories are on mountaintops, well away from city lights, with clear views of the sky above.*

Copernicus
(1473–1543)

Galileo
(1564–1642)

Newton (1642–1727)

Hubble (1889–1953)

◀ **Four famous astronomers.**
Copernicus was the first to say that the Earth circles the Sun. Galileo designed his own telescope. Newton discovered that the force of gravity keeps the Earth traveling around the Sun. Hubble's telescope showed him that galaxies are moving steadily apart.

▶ **The sighting of a comet** *is an exciting event. Comets are huge snowballs made of ice and dust. When they come close to the Sun, they develop tails of gas and dust that may be many hundreds of thousands of miles long.*

Traveling in Space

Spacecraft are blasted into space by powerful rockets. Once the rocket has used up its fuel, the spacecraft carries on under its own power.

The first living thing to travel in space was a dog named Laika, in 1957. The first person in space was Russian Yuri Gagarin, on April 12, 1961. He circled the Earth once. Just a few weeks later, Alan Shepard became the first U.S. astronaut (space traveler). His space flight lasted just 15 minutes. Astronauts today live and work in space, sometimes for months on end. Because there is so little gravity in space, everything in a spacecraft floats, including the astronauts.

◐ **A space shuttle** is a reusable spacecraft. It rides on a huge fuel tank to take off, uses its own power in space, and lands back on Earth like a plane. Shuttles are used to take astronauts to a space station.

WHAT DO ASTRONAUTS EAT?

Most space food is dried, to save weight. Water is added to the food packets before they are heated. Astronauts have to hold on to their food, otherwise it just floats around the spacecraft. All knives and forks are magnetic, so that they stick to the metal meal trays.

◖ **Astronauts can travel** *a short distance away from their spacecraft by putting a special jet-unit on their backs. They can move or turn in any direction using this Manned Maneuvering Unit (MMU).*

◖ **In 1969,** *American astronauts visited the Moon for the first time. They landed in a lunar module and wore spacesuits to walk on the Moon's surface. The suits protected them, provided them with air to breathe, and kept them at the right temperature.*

23

The Air

The Earth is surrounded by a blanket of air, called the atmosphere. Air is very important: without it, there would be no rain—in fact no weather—and no life.

The atmosphere is made up of many gases, including nitrogen and oxygen. We need to breathe oxygen to stay alive. High up in the atmosphere, a gas called ozone provides a barrier to harmful radiation from the Sun. Mars has an atmosphere a hundred times thinner than Earth's. Mercury has almost no atmosphere at all.

⬥ **The air gets thinner** *the higher you go. So on top of a very high mountain breathing is hard work. Mountaineers sometimes carry oxygen, to make breathing easier, when climbing at great heights.*

PROJECT

HEAVY AIR

Tie two balloons to the ends of a stick. Hang the stick from a piece of string so that it balances. Then blow up one of the balloons, and try to balance the stick again. You'll find it won't balance properly, because the air in the blown-up balloon makes it weigh more and so pushes that end down. This simple experiment shows that air has weight.

◑ **Wind is moving air.** *Sometimes whirling winds form a spinning funnel of air called a tornado. These extreme winds can destroy anything in their path.*

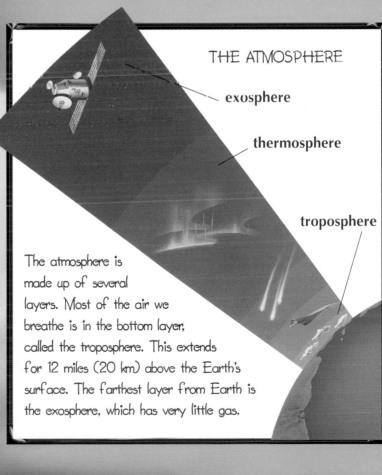

THE ATMOSPHERE

exosphere

thermosphere

troposphere

The atmosphere is made up of several layers. Most of the air we breathe is in the bottom layer, called the troposphere. This extends for 12 miles (20 km) above the Earth's surface. The farthest layer from Earth is the exosphere, which has very little gas.

Inside the Earth

Our planet Earth is a large ball of rock and metal covered with water and soil. The Earth is made up of four layers. The thin outer layer, called the crust, is the Earth's skin—like the peel of an orange. Beneath the crust is a thick layer, called the mantle, which is made of hot, molten (melted) rock. Near the center of the Earth are the two layers of the planet's core, which are made of metal.

The Earth's crust is cracked into huge pieces that fit together like a giant jigsaw puzzle. These pieces are called plates. The oceans and continents (landmasses) lie on the plates, which float on the mantle.

◐ **Earth looks cool** *from space, because of its water. Inside, the center is hot. It is nearly 4,000 miles (6,000 km) from the surface to the center.*

PROJECT

PLANET EARTH PUZZLE

Place a piece of tracing paper over the map on the opposite page. Trace the thick lines of the plates with a black felt pen, and add the outlines of the continents in pencil. Stick the traced map onto cardboard and color it in. Cut the map up into separate pieces to make your jigsaw puzzle. Jumble up the pieces, then use the plate lines to help you fit your puzzle together again.

The Earth's crust is the rocky layer beneath your feet.

The outer core is made of red-hot, molten iron and nickel.

The inner core is an iron ball. Although it is solid, this is the hottest part of the planet.

The mantle is so hot that the rocks have melted.

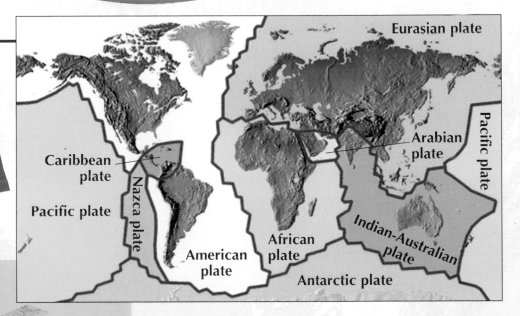

Eurasian plate

Caribbean plate

Arabian plate

Pacific plate

Pacific plate

Nazca plate

African plate

Indian-Australian plate

American plate

Antarctic plate

27

Volcanoes and Earthquakes

The plates that make up the Earth's crust slowly move and rub against each other. Though they only move a few inches each year, their buckling can cause volcanoes and earthquakes.

Volcanoes and earthquakes usually form near the edge of plates. Many of them happen in a region around the Pacific Ocean called the "Ring of Fire." They can cause giant waves called tsunamis.

The world's largest active volcano is Mauna Loa, in Hawaii. It rises to 13,680 feet (4,170 m) above sea level, and is over 30,000 feet (9,000 m) high when measured from the ocean bed. It erupts about once every four years. A volcano that has not erupted for a long time is

◑ **When a volcano** erupts, red-hot lava blasts up through an opening in the Earth's crust. The steep sides of a volcano are made of layers of hardened lava and ash. These layers build up with each eruption.

⬭ **Overpasses and bridges** *are at great risk when they are shaken by an earthquake. The quake's waves move out from a point called the epicenter. Very often there are minor tremors before and after a big earthquake.*

⬭ **The San Andreas Fault,** *in California, shows where two of the Earth's plates slide past each other. They move about 2 inches (5 cm) a year.*

said to be dormant, or "sleeping." If it has done nothing for thousands of years, it is said to be extinct.

The strongest recorded earthquake happened in Ecuador in 1906. It measured 8.6 on the Richter scale (the scale used to measure an earthquake's strength). A more recent earthquake killed 5,500 people in Japan in 1995.

SHAKEN BUT NOT DAMAGED?

The Transamerica Pyramid is a very tall building in San Francisco. It is 853 feet (260 m) high, and was specially designed to be able to survive earthquakes. Scientists and designers are always looking for new ways to make tall buildings safer for people.

Water

Water falls from clouds in the sky in the form of rain, snow, or hail.

When rainwater falls on the land, some of it seeps into the ground and is held in rocks below the surface. In limestone areas, this water makes underground caves. Some water collects in lakes, but most forms rivers that finally find their way to the sea.

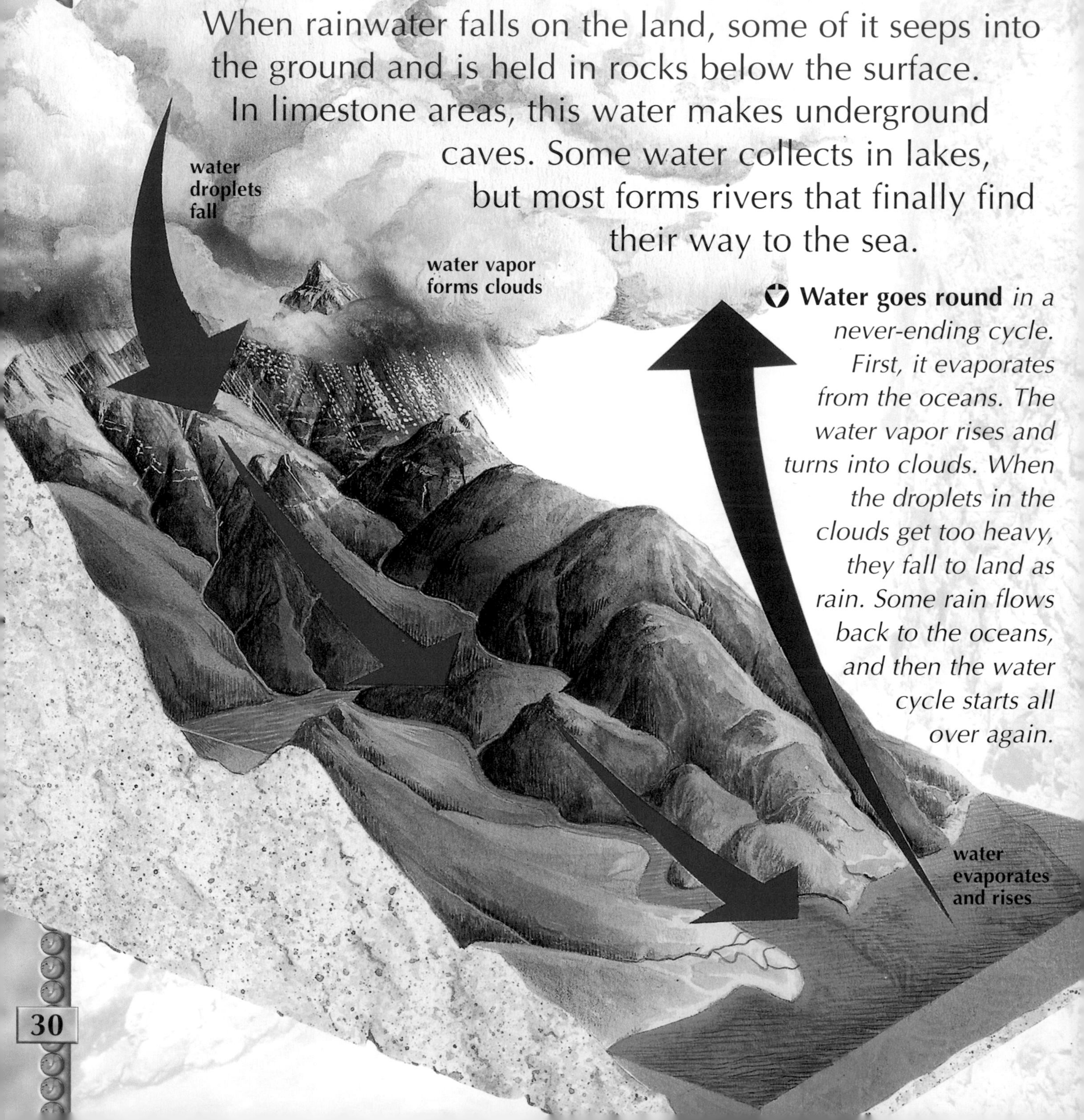

water droplets fall

water vapor forms clouds

⬙ **Water goes round** *in a never-ending cycle. First, it evaporates from the oceans. The water vapor rises and turns into clouds. When the droplets in the clouds get too heavy, they fall to land as rain. Some rain flows back to the oceans, and then the water cycle starts all over again.*

water evaporates and rises

◆ Most underground caves are made by running water. Over many years, rainwater wears away at cracks in soft limestone rocks. The cracks grow wider, making holes and then wide passages. Constantly dripping water creates fantastic rock shapes inside caves.

sinkhole

shaft

stalactite

stalagmite

cave

◆ **Where a river** drops over the edge of a hard rockface, it becomes a waterfall. Victoria Falls plunges 420 feet (130 m) on the Zambezi River in Africa.

MEASURING RAIN

PROJECT

To make your own rain gauge, pour a cup (200 ml) of water into a jar, 1 tbsp. at a time. Use a marker pen to mark tbsp. (10 ml) levels on the jar. Empty the jar, put in a funnel, and put the gauge outside to catch the rain.

Land and Sea

Millions of years ago, the Earth's land was made up of a single, huge continent (landmass). One big, deep ocean covered the rest of the planet.

Over millions of years, the original landmass split itself up into large pieces. As these pieces gradually moved farther apart, the Atlantic, Indian, and Arctic Oceans were formed. Today we call the remains of the huge stretch of water the Pacific Ocean.

200 million years ago

100 million years ago

today

Russia

North America

PACIFIC OCEAN

Australia

◗ **Viewed from space,** *the Earth looks like a very watery planet. The Pacific Ocean covers almost half the surface of the globe.*

◗ **The ocean floor** *has many similar features to dry land. There are mountains called seamounts and guyots, and valleys called trenches. A mid-ocean ridge is where new rock is made from molten rock beneath the Earth's surface.*

continental shelf

trench

guyot

seamount

◆ **This sea fan** *is a type of coral. Coral reefs usually form in the shallow waters around warm land. They are home to thousands of colorful plants and animals. The biggest coral reef in the world is the Great Barrier Reef, off the coast of Australia.*

◆ **The continents** *were once joined together as a giant supercontinent, called Pangaea. This split into two landmasses, and eventually separate continents formed. In order of size, the continents are: Asia, Africa, North America, South America, Antarctica, Europe, and Australasia. Together, they cover less of the Earth's surface than the Pacific Ocean. The continents are still moving apart, very slowly.*

SEA OF ISLANDS

PROJECT

Collect some stones and stick them together with modeling clay. Put your clay mountains in a plastic bowl and pour water in. As the bowl fills with water, islands form. It is easy to see that small islands are really the tops of underwater mountains. How many islands have you made?

mid-ocean ridge

At the Seashore

screw shell

Where an ocean meets land, waves pound against the shore and wear away the rocks in a process called erosion.

Cliffs of soft rock, such as white chalk, are worn away more quickly than hard rock. Waves grind rocks down into pebbles and sand, which are moved about as waves break on the seashore.

Twice a day, the water in the sea rises and goes down again. The tides are caused by the pull from the gravity of the Moon and the Sun. The world's biggest tides are found in the Bay of Fundy, in the Atlantic Ocean off Canada. There the water rises and falls up to 50 feet (15 m) between high and low tides.

⬧ **Rocks** *along the coast are worn away by wind and waves. This erosion forms pinnacles and stacks like this, called the Old Man of Hoy, in the Orkney Islands (UK).*

⬧ **The seashore** *teems with animals and plants that depend on the daily tides. Crabs often hide under rocks or seaweed. Lobsters live near rocky shores and move across the sea bed on four pairs of legs. Starfishes are related to sea urchins. They usually have five arms.*

lobster

crab

punctate
maurea

On rocky shores, *shellfish hide in their shells until the tide rises. The giant clam has the largest shell. It can grow up to 5 feet (1.5 m) across.*

giant clam

strawberry
top

spider
conch

starfish

Beautiful sandy beaches, *like this one in Hawaii, are a great favorite with vacationers all over the world. We don't think of these beaches as rocky, but grains of sand are really just very tiny pieces of broken rock and shells. Sand is popular with shellfish and other shore creatures too, because it is easy for them to dig into. Lugworms make the coiled tubes of sand that we sometimes see on the shore. The worms dig into the sand, eating it as they go for the tiny creatures it contains.*

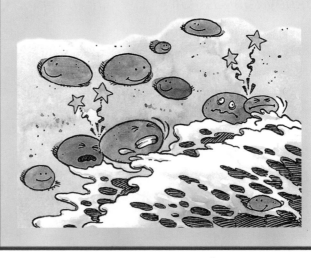

WHY ARE PEBBLES SMOOTH?

Big rocks break away from the land and fall into the sea. The rocks break up into smaller pebbles, and these knock against each other. Eventually they are worn smooth by being dragged up and down the shore by waves.

Mountains

There are high mountains all over the world. They took millions of years to form, as the plates that make up the Earth's crust pressed together and buckled.

Mountain ranges that lie near the edge of plates are still being pushed higher. They have steep, rocky peaks. Older ranges that lie farther from the plate edges have been worn away over the years by rain, wind, and ice.

The longest and highest mountain ranges, such as the Andes of South America and the Himalayas to the north of India, form huge mountain systems. Few animals or people live on the highest mountains. The ten highest mountains on land are all in the Himalayas. The highest peak of all, Mount Everest, lies on the border between Nepal and Tibet. It is 29,028 feet (8,848 m) high and is known to the people of Tibet as Chomolongma, or "goddess mother of the world."

WHAT IS AN IBEX?

The ibex is a wild mountain goat that lives in the high mountains in some parts of the world. Ibexes are sure-footed and happy to climb along rocky crags. Male ibexes have long horns, which they sometimes use to fight each other.

⬦ **Block mountains** *are created when the Earth's crust develops cracks, called faults, and the chunk of land between them is pushed up.*

The Earth's plates *are made up of layers of rock, called strata. As the plates move, the strata are bent into folds. On mountain rock-faces, you can often see how the layers have been folded into wavy lines.*

The longest mountain range *on land is the Andes, which stretches for over 4,000 miles (7,000 km) along the west coast of South America. The Transantarctic Mountains stretch right across the frozen continent of Antarctica.*

PROJECT

MOUNTAINS OF JUNK

Crumple newspaper into big balls and tape them onto a cardboard base. Make papier-mâché pulp by soaking newspaper pieces in a bucket of wallpaper paste. Cover the balls with the pulp to make mountains and valleys. When your landscape is dry, paint some snow-capped peaks with white paint. Sprinkle the base with sand. You could add a mountain lake.

Dome mountains *form when the top layers of the Earth's crust are pushed up by molten rock underneath. This makes a big bulge.*

Fold mountains *are formed when one plate bumps and pushes against another. Rock is squeezed up into folds. The Andes were made this way.*

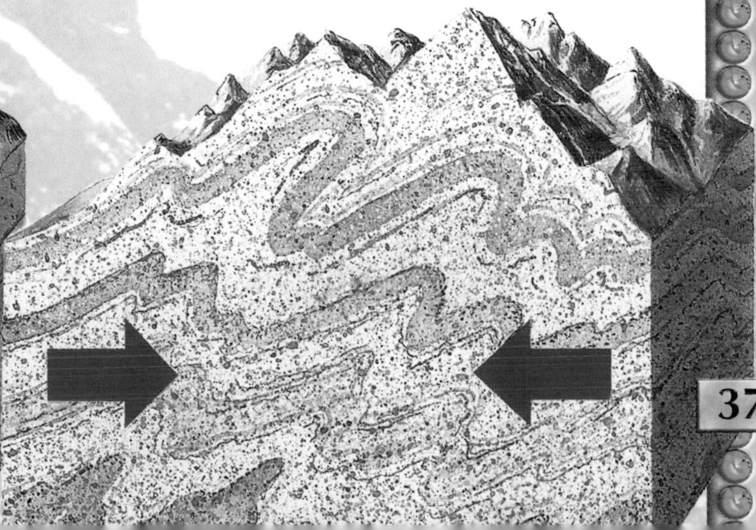

Rocks and Minerals

The Earth's crust is made up of rocks, and rocks are made of one or more minerals.

There are three main kinds of rock. Sedimentary rock forms when layers of sand, mud, and seashells pile up as a sediment and get squashed together.

◆ **Granite**, *an igneous rock, was used to build the Empire State Building in New York City. Granite is made up mainly of large grains of quartz, feldspar, and mica. It varies in color from gray to red, depending on the amount of these minerals present.*

MAKE A LEAF FOSSIL

PROJECT

Roll out a layer of clay and press a leaf firmly into it. Then carefully remove the leaf, which will leave behind its imprint. Make a cardboard ring, press it into the clay around the imprint, and pour liquid plaster of Paris over it. When the plaster is dry, take it out, peel off the clay and study your leaf fossil.

◆ **White cliffs** *are made of chalk. Chalk is a type of sedimentary rock, made from the shells of tiny sea creatures.*

Metamorphic rock is rock that has been changed by great heat and pressure. And igneous (or "fiery") rock is made when hot, melted rock from inside the Earth cools down and hardens.

Stage 1
Ammonites were sea creatures that died out about 65 million years ago. When an ammonite died, its body and coiled shell sank to the seabed.

Stage 2
Sediment made of sand and mud fell and built up around the ammonite. The animal's soft parts rotted, leaving just the shell.

Stage 3
Over millions of years the heavy sediment hardened into rock and the ammonite's shell was replaced by minerals. This left an outline of the creature's shell inside the rock.

Stage 4
The rock has been worn away by the weather to reveal the fossilized outline of the ammonite. Scientists can learn a lot about the ammonite from its fossils.

⬡ **This beautiful mineral** *is called selenite. It is a kind of gypsum, which is used to make plaster of Paris, cement, and school chalk.*

⬡ **How do fossils form?** *Fossils are the remains of living things, such as shells or sea creatures, preserved naturally in rocks.*

▶ **Marble** *is a metamorphic rock that forms when limestone is heated and squeezed. White marble is often used for sculpture.*

39

Forests

Almost a third of the Earth's land surface is covered with forests.

The trees that grow in forests vary according to the region's climate—how warm it is, how long the winter lasts, and how much rain falls in that region.

Cool northern forests are full of evergreen trees. Temperate forests have deciduous trees that lose their leaves in winter. And tropical rainforests have an enormous variety of big, fast-growing trees.

The taiga is the world's largest forest, stretching 6,000 miles (10,000 km) across northern Russia. The taiga is very cold during the long, dark winters, and summer in the forest is short and cool.

◄ **The massive sequoia trees** *in California are evergreen conifers. Some are thousands of years old. The largest is nearly 300 feet (90 m) tall, with a diameter of 36 feet (11 m). Imagine trying to climb to the top!*

◑ **The needle-leaved trees** of northern forests are called conifers. They bear their seeds in cones. Trees such as fir, pine, spruce, and larch have to survive long, cold winters there.

northern forest

MIGHTY OAKS

Some of the world's 600 or so kinds of oaks are quite small trees. Others, like the English oak, are massive. Oak trees live a long time, over 400 years, and oak wood is very hard and strong. The fruit of an oak tree is called an acorn.

oak leaf

◑ **Ash, beech, maple, and oak trees** all grow in temperate forests. In the fall, their leaves turn brown. Then they shed their leaves to save water and help them get through the winter.

temperate forest

◑ **Rainforests** grow on warm, wet lowlands, where it rains almost every day. Most rainforest trees are evergreen. Millions of creatures live in rainforests, as there is plenty of warmth, water, and food. In the tropical rainforests there are parrots and toucans, monkeys and jaguars, frogs and snakes. The Amazon rainforest in South America is the biggest tropical rainforest in the world. Parts are being cut down at an alarming rate.

rainforest

Deserts

Most deserts are in hot parts of the world, where it is dry nearly all the time.

Some deserts are covered with huge, high sand dunes. But there are many other desert landscapes, including rocky hills and stony plains. In the world's largest desert, the Sahara in northern Africa, the temperature often reaches 120°F (49°C).

Despite the heat and lack of water, deserts are not empty wastelands. Many have water underground. In places this water forms pools, called oases. Here plants can grow and people can live. The Sahara has about 90 large oases.

❂ In many desert regions, *rocks have been worn away over millions of years by the effects of heat and wind. The deserts of North America are full of strange-shaped, dramatic rock forms.*

PROJECT

BAKING DESERT

Mix smooth dough from 6 cups of flour, 3 cups of salt, and 6 tablespoons each of cooking oil and water. Roll the dough and shape it into a desert landscape. Bake the desert at the bottom of the oven at a low temperature for 40 minutes. When it has cooled down, paint with glue and sprinkle with sand. Paint a green oasis, and add tissue-paper palm trees and, perhaps, a clay camel for effect.

◀ **Cactus plants** store water in their fleshy stems. The giant saguaro cactus can grow over 55 feet (16 m) tall. Other desert plants shoot up suddenly if it rains, flower quickly, and scatter their seeds.

▼ **Some sand dunes** in the Sahara are 1,500 feet (450 m) high. Like waves in a sea of sand, they change and drift, blown by the wind.

Polar Regions

Near the North and South Poles, at the very top and bottom of the world, it is very cold.

The region around the North Pole is called the Arctic. Most of the Arctic region is a huge area of frozen sea, covered in thick ice. In winter the ice spreads over a wider area. The Arctic region also includes the north of Asia, Europe, and North America, where the frozen land is home to Arctic peoples such as the Inuit and the Lapps.

The South Pole is on the frozen land of Antarctica, which is the coldest continent on Earth.

There are icebergs in the cold sea near both Poles. The largest iceberg ever seen was about 200 miles (300 km) long and 65 miles (100 km) wide. It was in the South Pacific Ocean.

◑ *A glacier is a mass of ice that moves like a very slow river down a mountain. As a glacier flows downhill, it often cracks into deep openings called crevasses. In Antarctica, Lambert Glacier is over 400 miles (650 km) long. Antarctica's Ross Ice Shelf is the world's largest sheet of floating ice. It is about as big as France!*

◐ **Icebergs** *are huge chunks of floating freshwater ice that break off from glaciers and ice shelves. Only about a seventh of an iceberg appears above the water, so they are much bigger than they look.*

◗ **Norwegian explorer Roald Amundsen** *was first to reach the South Pole, in 1911. British explorer Robert Scott arrived a month later and found the Norwegian flag already flying there. At the South Pole, every way you look is north.*

◐ **The only people** *who live in Antarctica are scientists. Some live at a research station at the South Pole. Environmental teams, like these Greenpeace workers, also visit the Antarctic to study its climate, rocks, and animals. The continent is protected by an international treaty.*

Saving our Planet

Many of the Earth's most beautiful areas are in danger. Oceans, seashores, forests, and other regions are being overused and spoiled by people.

We can do a lot to help. Factories can stop pumping waste gases into the air and liquids into rivers. Most pollution comes from people trying to save money, instead of spending more to keep our planet clean.

◊ **Some factories** *pump dangerous gases into the air. These often get trapped in the atmosphere. Many scientists believe that this so-called "greenhouse effect" could be making the Earth warmer, having drastic effects on our planet.*

In some parts of the world, new sources of energy are being tried out. Solar panels collect energy directly from the Sun. Wind farms use windmill generators to make electricity. The power of the oceans' waves and tides are also being used in the same way.

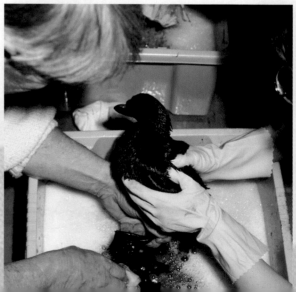

◑ **Oil spills** *from huge tankers can be very harmful to seabirds. They get clogged up with oil and then cannot fly or feed.*

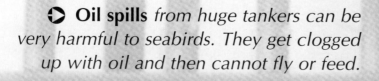

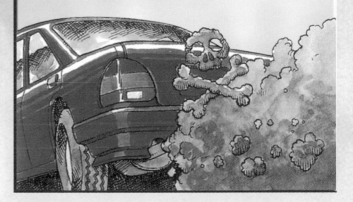

Most cars run on gasoline, which comes from oil. The world's oil is being used up, and car exhausts cause pollution. People can help the planet by walking and using trains and buses as much as possible.

Drink cans *may be crushed and recycled to make new cans. This saves energy and materials. Used glass bottles, paper, and clothes can also be collected and recycled.*

It's good for all of us *to plant new trees. They give out oxygen and so help make the fresh air that we breathe.*

Trees can be harmed *by a form of pollution called acid rain. This is caused by fumes from factories, power plants, and car exhausts, which contain dangerous chemicals. Some of the chemicals rise into clouds and later fall as acid rain.*

47

Quiz

1. What is the name of the planet on which we live? (page 10)
2. What is a round dent in a planet's surface called? (page 11)
3. How many planets travel around the Sun? (page 12)
4. Which planet is closest to the Sun? (page 12)
5. What is the name of our galaxy? (page 14)
6. Why do stars twinkle? (page 15)
7. Most scientists think the Universe began with a sort of explosion. What do we call it? (page 16)
8. Is our Sun the hottest star in the Universe? (page 17)
9. When a part of the Earth is tilted toward the Sun, is it summer or winter there? (page 18)
10. When do leaves turn brown and start to fall from the trees? (page 19)
11. What is a building that houses a big telescope called? (page 21)
12. Can you name one famous astronomer from the past? (page 21)
13. Who was the first living thing to travel in space? (page 22)
14. In which year did humans first step onto the Moon's surface? (page 23)
15. What is the name of the blanket of air around the Earth? (page 24)
16. Is air weightless? (page 25)
17. The Earth's crust is cracked into huge pieces. What are the pieces called? (page 26)
18. Which layer of the Earth lies just under the crust? (page 26)
19. Where is the world's largest active volcano? (page 28)
20. What is a tsunami? (page 28)
21. Do stalactites grow up from the floor of a cave, or hang down from the roof? (page 31)
22. Are the Victoria Falls in Africa or Europe? (page 31)
23. Which ocean covers almost half the globe? (page 32)
24. Which is the largest continent? (page 33)
25. What is the name for the rise and fall in the level of the sea? (page 34)
26. How many arms do starfish have? (page 35)
27. In which mountain range are the 10 highest mountains in the world? (page 36)
28. What is the name of the longest mountain range on land? (page 37)
29. What are white cliffs made of? (page 38)
30. What sort of animal was an ammonite? (page 39)
31. What sort of trees are fir, pine, and larch? (page 41)
32. What do we call the forests that grow on warm, wet lowlands near the equator? (page 41)
33. Most deserts have small areas with water where plants can grow. What are these areas called? (page 42)
34. Where do cactus plants store water? (page 43)
35. Where is the world's largest mass of floating ice? (page 44)
36. Who was the first explorer to reach the South Pole? (page 45)
37. What do solar panels collect their energy from? (page 46)
38. Why is it good to plant new trees? (page 47)

Science

Science is an exciting way of finding out about the world around us. What are things made of? How can we measure time? How do things work, and why do they work the way they do?

Scientists have been asking and trying to answer fascinating questions such as these and many others for thousands of years. They have invented machines to help them and make life easier. In recent times, television and the computer have changed the way many people live and work. Yet plants are just the same as they were centuries ago, and there is still a lot to learn about them, too. Science is knowledge, and science is fun.

Finding Out

The word "science" really means knowledge. It is all about finding things out.

We can start finding out by looking at things very carefully. We can look at plants and animals to see how they grow and change. We can look at rocks and fossils to see how the Earth developed. We can look at the stars to find out more about the Universe.

Scientists test things to see how they work. Their tests are called experiments, and they often involve measuring things. Scientists might measure size, weight, or time. When scientists test things, they keep a note of their results. This could be in a notebook, although, today, scientists often use computers to record their information.

◄ **Science** *helps our everyday lives. This researcher is using a microscope to study new medicines to help fight diseases.*
A microscope can make things look thousands of times bigger, so that you can see tiny details.

BEFORE AND AFTER

Try this simple experiment. Half-fill a measuring cup with water and note down the number of fluid ounces shown on the scale. Then put your hand in the water and see how far the water rises. Again, note down the fluid ounces shown on the jug. Ask a friend to do the same, and compare your results.

⚫ **A magnifying glass** *is like a simple microscope. You can use one to see things more clearly and closely, like the tiny markings on a caterpillar.*

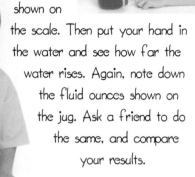

⚫ **The best way to find out** *about an animal and the way it behaves is to watch it carefully for some time. Afterward, you can find out more about it in an encyclopedia.*

⚫ **X-rays** *are pictures of the insides of things. This scientist is looking at an X-ray of a person's chest to check whether there is anything wrong inside, such as a broken bone.*

Time

When we are trying to find things out, time is very important. Scientists often need to measure how long it takes for things to happen.

The first clocks and calendars were invented thousands of years ago. They were based on the Earth's movements. We call one spin of the Earth a "day." And we call the time it takes for the Earth to travel around the Sun a "year."

🔻 **The Earth** *is divided into 24 time zones, one for each hour of the day. When it is 7.00 am in New York City, it is 12.00 midday in London, UK, and already 9.00 pm in Tokyo, Japan.*

candle clock

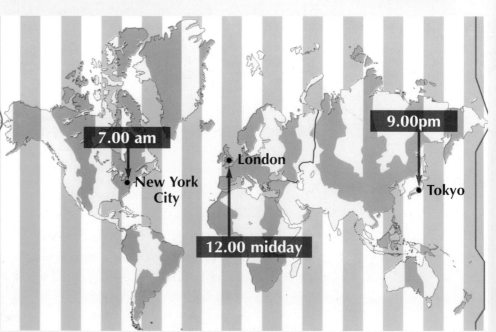

7.00 am

9.00pm

• London

• New York City

• Tokyo

12.00 midday

grandfather clock

The Earth *takes a year to travel around the Sun. We split this up into 12 calendar months of, usually, 30 or 31 days.*

The Moon *makes 12 trips around the Earth during a year. These are called lunar months. They do not add up exactly to one year.*

digital watch

hourglass

A sundial *is a type of shadow clock. The pointer's shadow moves around the dial as the Earth spins, pointing to the time. To us, it seems as if the Sun is moving across the sky.*

PROJECT

WATER CLOCK

Make a small hole in the bottom of a yogurt container. Attach a length of string to the pot and hang it up. Put another yogurt container under it. Then pour water into the hanging pot. Use a watch to time a minute and mark the water level on the bottom pot with a permanent marker. Carry on timing and marking more minutes. Then empty the bottom pot and refill the hanging pot. The marks on your water clock will now show you the passing minutes.

Materials

We use all sorts of materials to make things. Different materials are used to do very different jobs.

Metals are strong and are good at standing heat. Plastics don't break easily and can have lots of different colors. Glass is useful to see through and looks good. Wood has been used by people for thousands of years. Today it is still used to make furniture, as well as paper for books and magazines.

Look around and see how many kinds of materials you have in your home.

⬠ **Glass** *is transparent—it lets light through. This makes it useful for drink containers, because you can see what you are drinking. Light bulbs couldn't really be made of anything else!*

WHAT IF?

In the story of Cinderella, she wears a glass slipper. But imagine really doing that—or trying to bash in nails with a glass hammer! You need to use the right materials for the job.

⬠ **Many toys** *are made of plastic, because it is light, easy to clean, and does not break easily. It is a safe material for young children to play with.*

◆ **Many metals,** *when they are heated, become soft enough to be shaped into things—that is how spoons and safety pins are made. When they cool, they become hard again. A hammer would be no use if it was easily knocked out of shape.*

◆ **Plastics** *can be molded into all sorts of shapes. Most plastics will also bend quite easily. Many brushes are made entirely of this material. The first plastic was made by the American inventor John Wesley Hyatt, in 1868. It was called Celluloid. "Plastic" comes from a Greek word meaning "fit for molding."*

◆ **The glass walls** *of a greenhouse let the Sun's light and heat pass through. This is good for the plants inside. A wooden shed would keep out the light.*

◆ **Wood** *is generally a light but strong material, and can be carved into all sorts of shapes. Many things that once used to be made of wood are now made of plastic instead.*

Solids, Liquids, and Gases

Everything in the Universe, from the tiniest speck of dust to the biggest giant star, is made up of matter. This matter can take one of three forms: solid, liquid, or gas.

A solid is a piece of matter that has a definite shape. Wood is a hard solid, and rubber is a soft solid. A liquid, such as water, does not have a definite shape, but takes the shape of its container. A gas, such as air, also has no shape, and spreads out to fill its container.

◆ **A diver moves in liquid (water).** *The air cylinders the diver wears are solid. The air inside is a mixture of gases. As air is released, it bubbles to the surface, because air is lighter than water.*

◗ **You can fry** *a runny raw egg until it goes solid, but you can't unfry it!*

If you pour water *into an ice cube tray and put it in the freezer, the liquid becomes solid ice. If you then heat the ice cubes, they become liquid again.*

When the water boils, it turns to a gas called steam. And when the steam touches a cool glass mirror and loses heat, it changes back to water!

Red-hot lava *comes shooting out of a volcano as a liquid. The lava cools and turns into solid rock. Whether the lava is liquid or solid depends on how hot it is.*

SLOW FREEZER

PROJECT   Salty water does not freeze as easily as fresh water. To test this, dissolve as much salt as you can in a tin-foil container of cold tap water. Then put this in the freezer, along with another container of cold tap water. You will find that the fresh water turns to solid ice much faster than the salty water. This is because the salty water freezes at a much lower temperature.

CAN WATER FLOW UPHILL?

No, water always flows downhill. This is because it is pulled by the force of gravity, just like everything else. Water settles at the lowest point it can reach.

Energy

All the world's actions and movements are caused by energy. Light, heat, and electricity are all forms of energy. Our human energy comes from food.

Energy exists in many forms, and changes from one form to another. A car's energy comes from gasoline. When this is burned in a car, it gives out heat energy. This turns into movement energy to make the car go. Many machines are powered in this way by fuel.

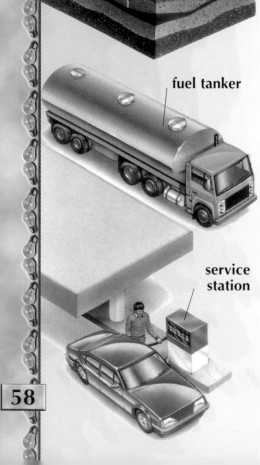

plant and animal remains

oil layer

oil well

fuel tanker

service station

◑ **Millions of years ago,** *the remains of dead sea plants and animals were covered by mud and sand. Heat and pressure turned these into oil, which was trapped between rocks. We drill down to the oil and bring it to the surface. We make gasoline from the oil, which we put into our cars. Then stored energy is turned into movement.*

◐ **When you hold a hot mug,** *the drink's heat passes through the mug and warms your hands. The mug is said to "conduct" heat.*

◑ **The hot water** *in a radiator warms the air, which in turn warms us. This movement of heat energy is called convection.*

WHAT A SHOWER!

Water in the home is heated by electricity or gas. We can save energy by not using more hot water than we need. A shower uses less hot water than a bath, so if we shower instead of bathing, we can save energy.

◊ The Sun heats the Earth and us *by radiation. On a summer's day, it is best to stay in the shade and drink a lot of water to stay cool.*

◊ All living things *on Earth get their energy from the Sun, which gives off light energy from 93 million miles (150 million km) away. The food chain shows how we use the Sun's energy. Grass and other plants turn the Sun's rays into food, so they can grow. Cows eat grass and use its energy to make milk, which we collect. When we drink the milk, we can use its energy to work, play, run, and jump!*

59

Electricity

Imagine what life would be like without the form of energy called electricity. You would not be able to make light or heat by flicking on a switch, and most of the machines in your home would not work!

The electricity we use at home is made in power stations. These can be powered by water, nuclear reactors, or fuel such as coal, oil, or natural gas. The electricity flows through wires from the power station to our homes. We call this flow an electric current. When you turn on a light switch, a current flows to the bulb and makes it work.

Another form of electricity does not flow through wires. It is usually still, or "static."

WARNING!

Never touch or play with plugs, sockets, wires, or any other form of electricity. You will get an electric shock and this could kill you.

 Static electricity *from a special generator can make your hair stand on end! You can make this happen at home, too, by combing your hair quickly, especially on a cold, dry day. An ancient Greek named Thales discovered static electricity over 2,500 years ago, when he rubbed a piece of amber with a cloth.*

Lightning *is a form of static electricity. The electricity builds up inside storm clouds, and then jumps from cloud to cloud or from the cloud to the ground as brilliant flashes of lightning. The flash makes a booming noise— thunder. We hear this after we see the flash, because light travels much faster than sound.*

STATIC BALLOONS

PROJECT Blow up a balloon. Rub it up and down on a shirt. The rubbing makes static electricity on the plastic skin of the balloon. Hold the balloon against your clothes and let go. Does the balloon stick? Now try holding it against your hair! You can also try using the static to pick up small pieces of tissue paper.

Magnets

A magnet pulls metal objects such as nails toward itself, with a power called magnetism.

Every magnet has two ends, called its north and south poles. The north pole of one magnet pulls the south pole of another toward it. This is useful in magnetic compasses, which we can use to find our way around the world because the Earth itself is a giant magnet. It has strong forces at the North Pole and the South Pole.

☉ The metal objects *below are all magnetic. If you put a magnet near them, they will move toward it. Objects made of wood or plastic are not magnetic. You could collect a group of objects and try them out with a magnet.*

MAGNETIC POLES

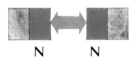

N   N

Try putting two magnets near each other. Same poles (north and north, or south and south) repel each other.

Different poles (north and south) attract each other.

N   S

◐ **A compass** *helps people find their way. The compass needle is a tiny magnet, and will always point north, toward the North Pole. By lining up the letter N (north) with the black tip of the needle, the person holding the compass can also see where east (E), west (W), and south (S) lie.*

Magnets are useful for doing many other things, too, from picking up cars to keeping fridge doors closed. But make sure that you keep magnets away from videos, cassette tapes, and computer disks. The effects of magnetism could damage them.

Another use of magnetism is in electromagnets. An electromagnet is a very powerful magnet. It is made by winding a wire around iron and passing electricity through it. This makes the wire magnetic.

◑ **Huge magnets** *are used in scrapyards to move chunks of scrap metal. This crane uses an electromagnet, which only works when the electricity is switched on. When the crane driver switches it off, the metal drops from the magnet.*

👁 **PROJECT**

FLOATING COMPASS

Stroke a needle with a magnet about 50 times in the same direction. The needle will become magnetic. Tape the needle to a piece of cork. Float the cork in a bowl of water, and you will see after a while that the needle settles and always points in the same direction—north.

Forces

Forces push or pull things. By doing this, they make things start or stop moving, speed up or slow down, change direction, bend or twist.

You put a pushing force on the pedals of your bike when you ride it, and the chain and wheels change this force to one that moves the bike along the road. A rubbing action called friction stops things from sliding. When you pedal your bike, you are working against the friction of the road on your tires. If you ride uphill, you are working against two forces—friction and gravity.

Gravity stops us from floating off the planet into space.

Everything that moves has a force acting on it. So without forces nothing would ever happen!

LEVERS

A lever multiplies the force we use to move a weight. A crowbar or pair of pliers works because the farther away from your hands the force is used, the bigger it is.

pliers

crowbar

◆ **A floating object,** *such as a sailboat, pushes water out of the space it takes up. The water pushes back. When the two pushes are balanced, the boat floats. The force of the wind on the sails pushes the boat along.*

◆ **The force of gravity** *pulls everything down to Earth. If you throw a ball up in the air, it will always stop and drop back down. If you're a good shot, it drops into the basket!*

◆ **A tug of war** *is a battle of pulling forces between two sets of human muscles. If the pull on one side of the rope is the same as the pull on the other side, no one wins. If one team is able to exert greater force, they will pull the other side toward them.*

Light and Color

Light is the fastest moving form of energy. Sunlight travels to Earth through space as light waves. We see things when light reflected from them travels to our eyes.

Light seems to us to be colorless, but really it is a mixture of colors. These are soaked up differently by various objects. A banana lets yellow bounce off it and soaks up the other colors, so the banana looks yellow.

Shadows are dark shapes. They are made when something gets in the way of light and blocks it out. This happens because light travels in straight lines and cannot bend around corners.

In this book, all the colors you see on the pages are made of a mixture of just four colored inks—blue, red, yellow, and black.

🔺 **The curved lens** *in a magnifying glass bends light, making things look bigger. By moving the position of the glass, you can see things the size you want.*

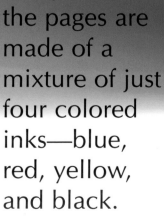

SPINNING COLORS

PROJECT

Here's a way to mix the colors of the rainbow back together. Divide a cardboard disk into seven equal sections. Color the sections with the seven colors of the rainbow (see opposite page). Push a sharpened pencil through the middle of the disk and spin it fast on the pencil point. The colors will all mix back to a grayish white.

◐ **Look in a mirror** *and you see a reflection of yourself. Light bounces back to you to make a wrong-way-round image. You can also see your reflection in still water.*

◑ **A rainbow** *shows sunlight in seven different colors. This happens when sunlight passes through raindrops and gets split up. Starting with the outer circle, the colors of a rainbow are red, orange, yellow, green, blue, indigo, and violet. The colors always appear in the same order.*

◓ **Light normally travels** *in straight lines. The plastic lenses in glasses change the direction of light and help people who need them to see things more clearly.*

◑ **If you pass a beam of light** *through a triangular piece of glass, called a prism, the light is split up into its different colors, just like a rainbow. The band of rainbow colors is called the spectrum of light.*

Sound

All sounds are made by things vibrating, or moving backward and forward very quickly.

Sound travels through the air in waves. It moves at a speed of about 740 mph (1,200 km/h). That's 30 times quicker than the fastest human runner, but almost a million times slower than the speed of light! A supersonic jet can fly at twice the speed of sound.

Our ears pick up sound waves traveling in the air around us. Sounds can move through other gases too, as well as through liquids and solids. So you can hear sounds when you swim underwater.

Dogs can hear both lower and higher sounds than people can.

HIGH AND LOW

A high-pitched whistle makes a higher sound than a big horn. A big cat makes a booming roar, while a mouse makes a high-pitched squeak. That's because they make different vibrations. The quicker something vibrates, the higher the sound it makes.

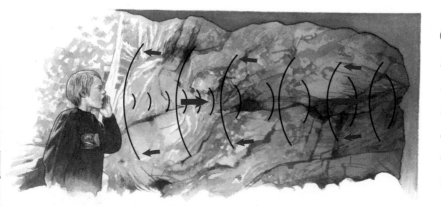

Sound waves *sometimes bounce back to you off a hard surface. When this happens, the sound makes an echo. A cave or a long corridor are good places to make an echo.*

LOUD AND QUIET

Bigger vibrations make bigger sound waves and sound louder. We measure loudness in decibels. Leaves falling gently on the ground might make 10 decibels of noise. A jet plane taking off makes about 120 decibels.

Bats and dolphins can make and hear even higher-pitched sounds, and use this ability to find their way around.

Astronauts on the Moon, where there is no air, cannot speak to each other directly and have to use radio.

WHY WEAR EAR MUFFS?

People who work with loud machines wear muffs to protect their hearing. This is because loud noises are painful to the ears and can damage them, especially if the noise goes on for a long time.

◆ **Sound travels** through the air. When you whisper in someone's ear, the sounds go into the ear. Cupping your hand stops the sound waves spreading, so your friend can hear even a whisper.

◗ **A guitar** makes sounds when you pluck the strings. The strings vibrate, or move backward and forward. If you press down hard on the strings, you stop the vibration and so you also stop the sound.

69

Cars and Bikes

Today's cars come in all shapes and sizes, from small city cars to big luxury vehicles. Most of them are built by robots. In the factory, the robots weld different parts together as car bodies move between them.

The cars are powered by engines that run on gasoline or diesel oil. To save energy and cut down on the pollution caused by exhaust fumes, new types of engines are being invented. Cars are also being made safer all the time.

Motorcycles take up less room on the road. Cycles use just human energy to power them along.

▶ **Motorcycle racing** *is a popular sport. Riders lean over as they take bends at great speed. This helps them keep their balance and go faster. The fastest motorbikes go at over 180 mph (290 km/h).*

◗ **In most cars,** *the engine is at the front, under the hood. It burns gasoline, to turn a shaft connected to the wheels. The car's battery stores electricity, and the radiator helps to cool the engine.*

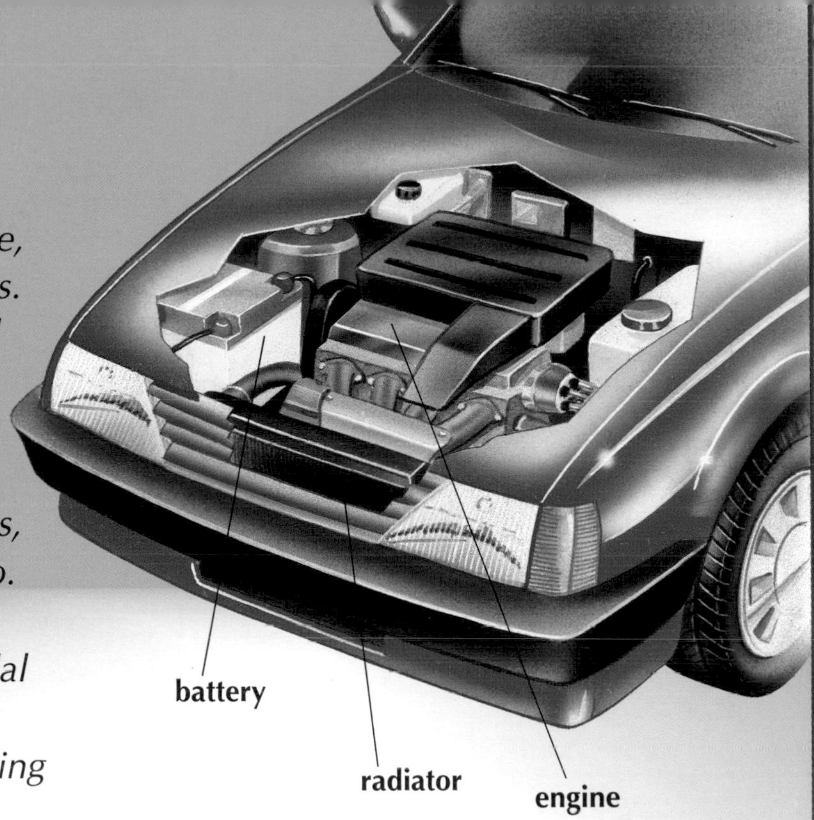

◗ **Mountain bikes** *are strong and fast. They are built for riding on rough trails, but are very popular on city roads, too. Your bike's gears allow you to ride slowly or more quickly while you pedal at a comfortable rate. A car's gears do the same job for the engine, by changing the speed of the wheels.*

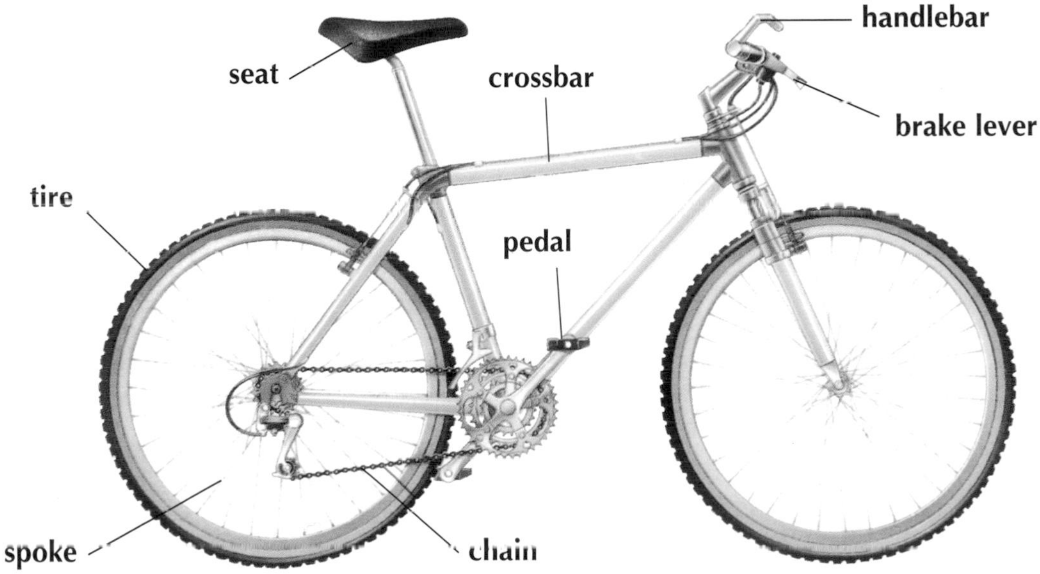

battery

radiator

engine

handlebar

seat

crossbar

brake lever

tire

pedal

spoke

chain

◗ **This car** *runs on the Sun's energy. Its flat shape helps solar panels to collect the energy. One day cars like this may drive on our roads and highways.*

Trains, Ships, and Planes

Trains carry people and goods in railway cars. They are pulled along their tracks by powerful locomotives.

Ships have sailed on the world's oceans and seas for thousands of years. Hundreds of years ago they helped people to discover new lands and settle in other parts of the world.

Some modern ships have water jets instead of propellers to push them along.

WHAT IS A MAGLEV TRAIN?

Maglev stands for magnetic levitation. A maglev train floats on a magnetic field and is driven by the effect of magnets. It has no wheels and travels along a guideway instead of on rails. Maglevs may well be the trains of the future.

The French TGV *high-speed electric train holds the world speed record for trains: 319 mph (515 km/h). Trains run along metal tracks, and electric trains pick up power for their motors from overhead wires or an extra rail in the track. There are also diesel-oil trains and a few old-fashioned steam trains.*

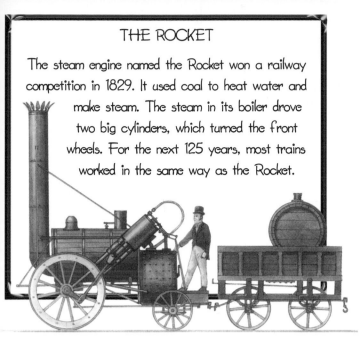

THE ROCKET

The steam engine named the Rocket won a railway competition in 1829. It used coal to heat water and make steam. The steam in its boiler drove two big cylinders, which turned the front wheels. For the next 125 years, most trains worked in the same way as the Rocket.

The jets drive out water under great pressure and can be turned to make the ship change direction.

The biggest ships are oil tankers, which can be more than 1,500 feet (453 m) long. They need a lot of room to turn around!

Jet planes are the quickest and cheapest form of long-distance transportation. Helicopters also fly, but use high-speed spinning blades instead of wings. They can hover in mid-air and land on small helipads on top of tall buildings, lighthouses, or oil rigs out at sea.

◐ **Cargo ships** *carry heavy loads such as fuel, timber, and containers (like the ones shown here) packed with goods. Ships are slow but can carry bigger loads than planes.*

◔ **Jet planes** *carry passengers around the world in a few hours. From 1976 to 2003, Concorde was the world's only supersonic airliner. It could fly at 1,200 mph (1,900 km/h) but had room for fewer people than the bigger, slower jumbo jets, which can carry over 400 passengers.*

Technology in the Home

Today most people have a lot of helpful machines in their homes. The machines are there to make life easier and to save people time. Most of them are powered by electricity.

Housework is much easier now than it has ever been. Before people had washing machines, they spent hours washing their clothes by hand. Now it just takes a few minutes to fill the machine and set the right wash program.

Home technology means that people have more time—to work or to relax.

◀ **A hairdryer** sucks air in at the back, warms it as it passes through, and then blows the warm air out through the nozzle at the front. It dries hair much faster than a towel!

◀ **A vacuum cleaner** sucks up dust and dirt in a current of rushing air. The dirt is deposited in a bag that has to be emptied. This kind of cleaner was invented in 1908, in the USA. The more recent, more efficient bagless cleaners suck air into a cylinder and spin it at high speed. The dirt is thrown out of the air into a plastic container.

▶ **A microwave oven** cooks food very quickly by sending invisible waves of energy, called microwaves, into the food. This makes the watery parts of the food vibrate and get hot.

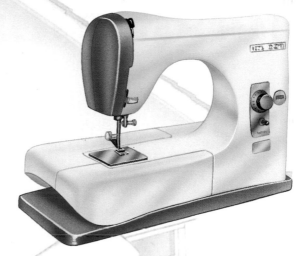

● **The first sewing machines** *in the 1800s were worked by a person turning a wheel by hand, or pushing a foot-pedal up and down. Modern sewing machines like this one have electric motors to do the work.*

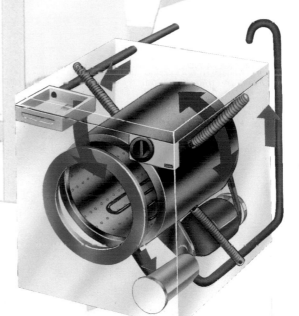

● **A refrigerator** *keeps food cold by removing heat from inside the cabinet. A liquid flows around pipes at the back of the refrigerator. The liquid changes to a gas and takes up heat from inside the cabinet. The pipes give off the heat behind the refrigerator.*

● **A washing machine** *is a simple electrical device. It works by mixing dirty clothes up with soapy water. A drum inside the machine turns to slosh the clothes in the water, and then clean water rinses away the soap and dirt. Finally, the machine's drum spins very fast, to help dry the clothes.*

Computers

disk drive

Computers can do all sorts of different jobs for us, easily and very quickly. Many people use computers at home, as well as at work and at school.

We can use computers to write letters and reports, store lots of information—such as lists or addresses—do complicated math, or design things.

Most of the work you do on a computer can be seen on its screen. You can also print work out on paper.

keyboard

disks

CDs

◆ **When you put on a** virtual-reality headset, you enter a pretend world created by a computer. Inside the headset are two small screens, showing you pictures that look real. If you use a special glove to touch things, the computer reacts to every move you make. The system can be used by air traffic controllers to see planes as if they were real and give commands to tell them what to do.

WHAT IS E-MAIL?

It stands for electronic mail, a way of sending messages between computers all over the world. You write a letter on your computer, then send it down a telephone line to someone else's computer, instantly. In comparison, ordinary post is so slow that e-mailers call it "snail mail."

You can use a keyboard *and a mouse to put information into the computer. Then you can store your work on a disk, as well as inside the computer itself.*

There are lots *of exciting computer games. You play many of them by using a joystick.*

screen

mouse

STRINGING ALONG

PROJECT

To make your own phone system, make a hole in the bottom of two plastic or paper cups, or yogurt containers. Then thread a long piece of string through the holes and tie a knot at each end, inside the cup. Ask a friend to pull the string tight and put a cup to his ear. Now speak into your cup and he will hear you. It's as fast as e-mail!

TV and Radio

The world's first radio broadcast was made in the USA in 1906. The first proper TV service began in 1936 in London. At that time there were just 100 television sets in the whole of the UK!

Today many people spend hours each day watching TV or listening to the radio. Along with newspapers and magazines, TV and radio provide us with entertainment and information.

⬆ **A television set** *receives electrical signals, which it changes into pictures. It fires streams of particles onto the back of the screen. These build up a picture, and this changes many times each second. South Korea makes more color television sets than any other country: over 16 million every year!*

⬇ **For satellite TV,** *a program is transmitted to a satellite in space. The signal is then beamed back to Earth by the satellite and is picked up by dishes on people's homes. Their television set changes the signal back into pictures.*

TV studio

transmitter

satellite

dish

◀ **Camera operators** *in a TV studio use video cameras to record new programs. The cameras are bigger, more complicated versions of the camcorders that people use at home.*

WHAT DOES TELEVISION MEAN?

"Tele" means far, so television simply means "far sight." When we watch TV, we are seeing things that are far away. A telescope is a "far-seeing instrument," and a telephone is a "far sound"!

Television signals can be received by an antenna or by a satellite dish. Some people have TV signals brought straight into their homes through a cable. In most countries there are many different channels and programs to choose from, day and night.

▶ **A radio telescope** *is used to send and receive radio waves. Both radio and TV signals travel as radio waves. Astronomers also use radio telescopes to pick up signals from parts of space that we can't see through other telescopes. The largest radio telescope in the world is at Arecibo, on the Caribbean island of Puerto Rico. The dish is 1,000 feet (305 m) across and stands inside a circle of hills.*

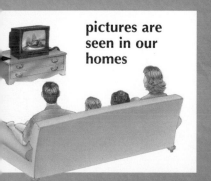

pictures are seen in our homes

79

Plants

Living plants are found almost
everywhere where there is sunlight,
warmth, and water. They use
these to make their own food.

Plants have a special way of
using the Sun's energy, with a green
substance in their leaves called
chlorophyll. They take in a gas called
carbon dioxide from the air and mix it
with water and minerals from the soil.
In this way they make a form of
sugar, which is their
food. This whole
process is called
photosynthesis.

flower

stem

fruit

leaf

roots

◁ **The
leaves and
flowers** *of
water lilies float on
the surface of the water. We call
the leaves lily pads. The plants'
stems are under the water, and
their roots are in the mud and soil
at the bottom of the pond. The
pads of some large water lilies
grow over 6 feet (2 m) across.*

▷ **A plant's roots** *grow
down into the soil. They
are covered in tiny hairs,
which take in water and
minerals. Water moves
through the stem to the
leaves, which make the
plant's food.*

midrib

vein

tip

bud

stem

inside a leaf

Leaves take in carbon dioxide gas through tiny holes on their underside. They also give out oxygen, which other living creatures, including people, breathe. So leaves keep us alive. The largest leaves of any plant grow on palm trees on islands in the Indian Ocean. The leaves are up to 65 feet (20 m) long.

Cacti live in hot, dry regions, such as deserts. They store water in their fleshy stems. Their leaves are in the shape of sharp spines, which help protect them from desert animals.

Some bromeliads live on other plants in the rainforest. They grow in pockets of soil that form in the bark of trees. Their roots dangle freely and take in most of their moisture from the damp forest air.

Ferns reproduce by means of tiny cells called spores, seen here under a microscope. There are about 10,000 different kinds of ferns. They like damp places.

SUN BLOCK

PROJECT

Cover a patch of green grass with an old can or saucer—but not on someone's prize lawn! Lift the can after a few days and you will see that the grass is losing its color. After a week, it will be very pale. This is because it couldn't make food in the dark. Take the tin away and the grass will soon recover.

Flowers

People grow flowers so that they can enjoy their colors, shapes, and perfume. But flowers are more than just pretty. They have an important job to do for their plants.

▷ **Some plants** *have many small flowers on one stem, while others have one big flower. The petals do not usually last long. Once they have attracted animals to pollinate the plant, they drop off.*

Flowers make the seeds that grow into new plants. Male parts of the flower produce pollen grains. When these reach the female parts, they fertilize eggs, to make seeds. Birds, insects, and other animals often help this process by feeding on flowers and moving the pollen grains. This process is called pollination.

carpel { stigma
         style

petal

anther } stamen
filament

◐ **A flower** *has male and female parts—stamens and carpels. The stigma at the top of the style catches pollen grains, which reach down the style to meet egg cells and make seeds.*

♤ **There are almost 20,000** *types of orchid. Their seeds are so light they can be blown over 600 miles (1,000 km) by the wind.*

◆ **It is easy to see** how beautiful, colorful flowers attract insects and other animals. Many flowers can be found in all sorts of different colors. These chrysanthemums are just one of more than 200 different types of this popular garden flower.

◆ **Some trees,** such as birch and hazel, have flowers that hang down like loose tassels. These flowers, called catkins, often appear before the tree's leaves each spring. The pollen on the catkins is easily blown by the wind, so that it moves from flower to flower and tree to tree.

◆ **A hummingbird** can hover in front of a flower while it feeds on the sweet nectar. Pollen sticks to its long beak and is carried to the female part of the plant or to another plant when the bird next feeds. The same thing happens with bees, when they collect nectar to make honey. They find flowers by their color and scent. Some bats also feed on nectar, in the same way as hummingbirds. The bats have long, tubelike tongues.

Trees

Trees are not only among the largest living things on Earth; they are also the longest living. The oldest trees on Earth are bristlecone pines in the U.S. Southwest. Some are over 5,000 years old.

A tree trunk is really just a hard, woody stem. Under the protective bark, water and food travel up through the outer layer of wood, called the sapwood, to the tree's crown of branches and leaves.

Fine roots take in the water, but trees have big, strong roots as well. These help anchor the trees firmly in the ground.

Mangrove trees grow in swamps and are the only trees to live in salty water.

◐ **The tamarind** *has beautiful leaves. It is an evergreen tree that grows in warm regions to a height of 80 feet (24 m).*

◑ **The leaves of birch trees** *are shaped like triangles, with toothed edges. In the fall, they turn brown before falling from the tree. Native Americans used the bark of birch trees to make canoes.*

⬙ Trees grow a new ring *of wood every year. If there is lots of sunshine and rainfall, that year's ring is wide. You can count the rings of a felled tree to see how old the tree is.*

growth ring

bark

heartwood

⬙ As an oak tree grows *and the trunk widens, its bark breaks up into pieces like a jigsaw puzzle. In the middle is a core of dark brown heartwood.*

⬙ Different leaves *do different jobs. Small leaves, like these fir tree needles, lose less water than broad, flat leaves. Big leaves show a larger surface area to the Sun and so are able to make more food. Many palm trees have large, fan-shaped leaves that grow straight out from the top of the trunk instead of from branches. Palms grow best in places where it is warm all year round.*

BARK PATTERNS

PROJECT

Every tree has a unique pattern on its bark. You can see these wonderful patterns by transferring them to paper. Just attach or hold a sheet of paper firmly against a tree trunk. Then carefully rub over the paper with a crayon until the bark pattern shows up. Bark rubbings make beautiful pictures. Try using different colored crayons to make unusual effects.

Fruit, Nuts, and Seeds

A **fruit is the part of a plant that protects and feeds new seeds as they grow. Berries and nuts are really different kinds of fruits.**

⬣ **The pips in apples** *are the seeds. We grow apple trees specially for their juicy fruit, and carefully plant the seeds ourselves.*

Some fruits are very light and are blown by the wind. Others fall to the ground, and have hard shells around the seeds to protect them. The world's largest seeds are those of coco-de-mer trees. Each of the huge heart-shaped seeds can weigh as much as

⬣ **A peach** *is a round fruit with a large, hard seed inside, called a stone or pit. Nectarines are a type of peach.*

⬣ **The cluster of seeds** *inside these slices of juicy water melon and kiwi fruit are easy to see. These fruits grow best in warm climates.*

GROW WATERCRESS

PROJECT

Wild cress grows in streams or on mud. You can easily grow cress seeds yourself on paper. Place two sheets of paper towel on a tray and wet this thoroughly. Put the tray on a window sill and keep it damp. In about 7 to 10 days you will be able to cut your own cress.

○ **Walnut** *are nuts from walnut trees. The wrinkled walnut is inside the hard outer shell. Nuts are rich in protein and fat.*

○ **Cherries** *are delicious small fruits surrounding a hard stone that contains a seed.*

45 pounds (20 kg).

Soft fruits are often eaten by animals. When a bird eats berries, the seeds usually pass through the bird's digestive system without being harmed. So without knowing it, the bird may later deposit the seeds in ground a long way away.

○ **Strawberries** *have tiny pips, which are actually the plant's true fruits. Wild strawberries are smaller than the strawberries sold in stores all year round.*

○ **Coconuts** *are the fruit of the coconut palm. They can float, and so can be carried long distances by the sea, to land and take root on a faraway beach. The watery liquid inside coconuts is called coconut milk. It makes a refreshing drink.*

Quiz

1. What are scientists' tests called? (page 50)

2. What can you use to see things more clearly and closer up? (page 51)

3. How long does it take for the Earth to travel around the Sun? (page 53)

4. How many trips around the Earth does the Moon take in a year? (page 53)

5. What material was Cinderella's shoe made of? (page 54)

6. Which material comes from a Greek word meaning "fit for molding?" (page 55)

7. What does a liquid take the shape of? (page 56)

8. What happens to ice cubes when you heat them? (page 57)

9. Where do all living things get their energy from? (page 59)

10. Which uses less water, a bath or a shower? (page 59)

11. Which form of electricity does not flow through wires? (page 60)

12. Which comes first, thunder or lightning? (page 61)

13. What are the two ends of a magnet called? (page 62)

14. Which magnetic instrument helps people find their way? (page 63)

15. Which force pulls everything down to Earth? (page 64)

16. Which of these is not a lever—crowbar, battery, pliers? (page 65)

17. What is the fastest moving form of energy? (page 66)

18. Can you name the colors of the rainbow? (page 67)

19. Where are good places to make an echo? (page 68)

20. Why do some workmen wear ear muffs? (page 69)

21. What do most car engines run on? (page 71)

22. What does a car's radiator do? (page 71)

23. What does maglev stand for? (page 72)

24. What is the name of the world's only supersonic passenger airliner? (page 73)

25. Is it quicker to dry your hair with a hairdryer or a towel? (page 74)

26. What turns inside a washing machine? (page 75)

27. What do you store your computer's work on? (page 77)

28. What does the "e" in e-mail stand for? (page 77)

29. How does satellite television work? (page 78)

30. Where is the world's largest radio telescope? (page 79)

31. What is the name of the green substance in plants? (page 80)

32. Where do cacti live? (page 81)

33. How far can an orchid's seeds be blown by the wind? (page 82)

34. Which birds hover in front of flowers while feeding? (page 83)

35. What do a tree's roots do? (page 84)

36. Which trees have no branches? (page 85)

37. What are apple pips? (page 86)

38. Which tree produces the largest seeds in the world? (page 86)

Human Body

The human body is made up of many different parts, big and small, simple and complex, from the bony skeleton to the hard-working heart. These parts all work together to make us a whole person, helping us to live and keeping us healthy. Watching over all the parts is our control center, the brain.

We have a great deal to learn about ourselves and how our bodies work. This includes how we were born and what happens to us as we grow older. We can learn how to look after ourselves and others, too, so that we live happy, healthy lives.

head

hand

neck

arm

Parts of the Body

Men and women, boys and girls are all human beings. Our bodies are all similar, though no two people look exactly the same. The human body is made up of many parts, each having its own special job to do. These different parts are all controlled by the brain, which also enables us to think and move. Our senses of sight, hearing, touch, taste, and smell help us in our daily lives. To work properly, our bodies need energy, which we get from our food.

torso

leg

foot

nucleus

cell membrane

◀ **The largest part** *of the body is called the torso, or trunk. The four limbs are joined to the torso. The hands at the ends of our arms help us touch and hold things. Our feet help us stand upright and walk. The head is on top of the neck, which can bend and twist. The brain is inside the head. Two thirds of the body's weight is made up of water. The body also contains carbon, calcium, and iron.*

cytoplasm

◐ **We have many large organs** *inside our bodies. These are parts that do special jobs for the rest of the body. Organs work together to make up different body systems.*

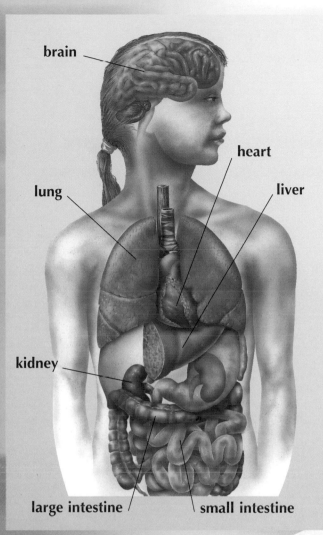

brain

heart

liver

lung

kidney

large intestine

small intestine

BODY SHAPES

PROJECT

To draw body shapes, you need some very big pieces of paper. Put the paper on the floor and ask a friend to lie on it. Draw around him or her with a pencil. Then take the paper away and cut out the outline shape. You can draw on a face and any other features you want, before pinning the picture up on the wall. Then you could ask a friend to draw your shape.

◐ **We all begin life as one single cell.** *This divides into two. These cells also divide, and so on, until there are billions of cells, each one so small that it can only be seen through a microscope. Most cells have three main parts. In the middle is a nucleus, the control center that helps make new cells. This is surrounded by a soft fluid called cytoplasm. The outer surface of the cell is called its membrane. Similar types of cells join together to make tissue.*

skull

Skeleton

The skeleton is our framework of bones. Our bones provide a firm surface for muscles to attach to, helping us to move. An adult has about 206 bones. Babies are born with as many as 270 small, soft bones. As a child grows, some of the bones join together. The skeleton protects our body's organs. The skull protects the brain. Our heart and lungs are protected by the rib cage. The body's bones vary in shape and size. The places where they meet are called joints, which is where muscles move bones.

humerus

rib cage

vertebra

ulna

radius

pelvis

femur

tibia

fibula

● **Our spine, or backbone,** *is made up of 33 vertebrae. You may be up to half an inch shorter in the evening than early in the morning, because the weight of your upper body squashes your spine slightly as you stand and walk during the day. At the lower end of the spine is the pelvis. A woman's pelvis is wider than a man's, to make room for a baby. The lower parts of our arms and legs have two bones. The femur, or thigh bone, is the largest bone in the body.*

MOVING JOINTS

Joints let us move in different ways. The hip and shoulder are ball-and-socket joints. The knee and elbow are hinge joints. There is a pivot joint at the top of the spine, and a saddle joint at the thumb's base.

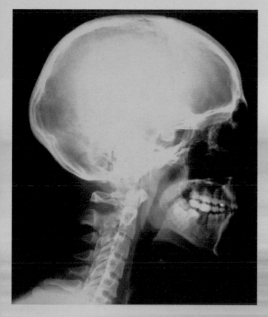

◐ **An X-ray photograph** allows doctors to see bones inside the body. They use X-rays to see if a bone is broken or damaged.

◐ **At the center of bones** is soft marrow. This is inside the toughest part, called compact bone, which is lined with spongy bone. A bone's outer layer is called the periosteum.

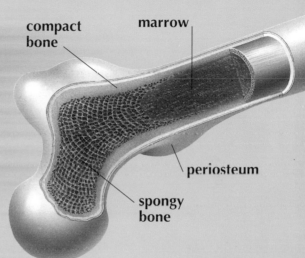

compact bone

marrow

periosteum

spongy bone

◐ **The skeletons of insects,** such as this beetle, are on the outsides of their bodies. They act like shells, covering and protecting the soft parts underneath, as well as protecting the insect from its enemies.

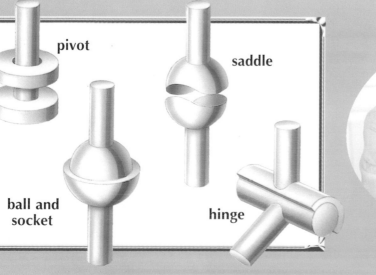

◐ **For a broken bone** to heal properly, the pieces have to be placed next to each other and kept still. That is why a doctor puts a broken arm or leg in a plaster cast. New bone tissue grows to join the broken bone ends together again.

pivot

saddle

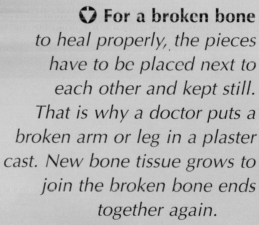

ball and socket

hinge

Muscles

All our movements, from running to blinking, are made by our muscles. The muscles work by becoming shorter and pulling the bones to which they are attached.

The human body has about 620 muscles that it uses for movement. Other muscles work automatically, such as those that make the heart beat, the chest muscles that help us breathe, and the stomach muscles that help us digest food.

Tiny muscles in the eyes help us to focus. These move about 100,000 times a day. You would have to walk about 50 miles (80 km) to give your leg muscles the same amount of exercise!

deltoid

back muscles

gluteus maximus

◀ **The body is moved** *by layers of muscles. The largest muscle is the gluteus maximus in the buttock.*

▶ **Athletes** *need very strong muscles. They do a lot of exercise and training to develop bigger and stronger muscles.*

hamstring

calf muscle

biceps

triceps

elbow

◐ **Because muscles** *can only pull as they shorten, they work in pairs. To lift something, the biceps muscle gets shorter and bends the hinge joint of the elbow. To put the object down again, the triceps muscle shortens and the biceps muscle lengthens.*

abdominal muscles

biceps

chest muscles

THE STRONGEST MUSCLES?

The strongest muscles in the human body are not in your arms or legs, but on each side of your mouth. They are the muscles that we use to bite. That's why it hurts so much if you accidentally bite your tongue!

◑ **There are large muscles** *near the surface under the skin, and others lie beneath them. Three layers of criss crossing abdominal muscles connect the rib cage to the pelvis.*

◐ **More than 30 small muscles** *run from the skull to the skin. These allow us to make facial expressions, which we use to show our feelings.*

sad

sartorius

shocked

happy

95

The Heart and Blood Circulation

The heart is a powerful muscle that pumps blood all around the body.

An adult body contains about 10 pints (5l) of blood. So every day an adult's heart pumps over 14,000 pints (7,000l) of blood around the body. The blood carries oxygen from the air we breathe and goodness from the food we eat.

The heart is pear-shaped and is about as big as your clenched fist. It lies in your chest, behind your ribs. If you put your hand over your heart, you can feel it beating.

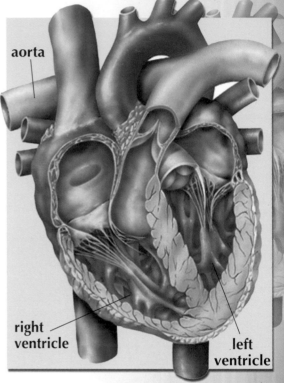

aorta

right ventricle

left ventricle

◆ **The right side** of the heart pumps blood to the lungs to pick up oxygen. The left side pumps the blood around the body.

YOUR HEART

Your heart has to work harder to pump blood upward, because then it is working against gravity. If you hold one hand up for a minute, you'll see that it has less blood in it afterward, and so is paler than the other hand.

👁 **PROJECT**

heart

◀ **Blood travels** *away from the heart in blood vessels called arteries. It travels back to the heart in veins. In this picture, arteries are shown in red and veins in blue.*

◆ **A doctor** *examines a young patient. Heart trouble is rare in children, but can affect older people. The heart is a very hardworking organ. The more energy you use, the harder your heart works.*

A child's heart rate is about 100 beats a minute. When you are running, your heart beats faster and your body's cells need more oxygen and food.

artery

vein

LISTEN TO THE BEAT

PROJECT

You can make your own stethoscope, so that you can easily listen to your own or a friend's heartbeat. Simply cut the top ends off two plastic bottles. Then push the ends of some plastic tubing into these two cups. Put one cup over a friend's heart and the other cup over your ear, and listen!

Breathing

Every time we breathe, we take in air containing a gas called oxygen. We need oxygen all the time to make our bodies work. The air we breathe in passes into our two lungs, which are well protected inside the rib cage. The lungs take oxygen from the air and pass it into our bloodstream. Our blood takes oxygen all around the body.

◑ **Runners** *need to get a lot of oxygen to their muscles very quickly. To achieve this, they breathe hard and their hearts beat quicker.*

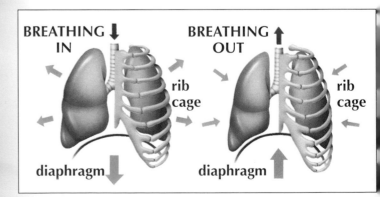

BREATHING IN ↓   BREATHING OUT ↑

rib cage   rib cage

diaphragm ↓   diaphragm ↑

◑ **As you breathe in,** *your rib cage expands and a large dome of muscle, called the diaphragm, flattens. When you breathe out, the diaphragm rises.*

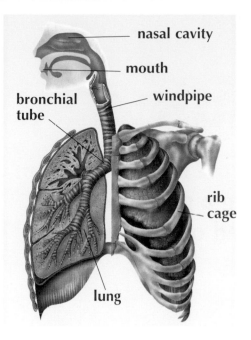

nasal cavity
mouth
bronchial tube
windpipe
rib cage
lung

◑ **The air we breathe in** *through the nose and mouth goes down the windpipe. This branches into two bronchial tubes, one for each lung. Inside the lungs, the tubes divide and get smaller. Oxygen passes from the tiniest tubes to blood vessels and finally into the bloodstream.*

When we breathe out, the lungs get rid of used air. Adults breathe about 18 times a minute (more than 25,000 times a day). Children usually breathe faster.

◗ **This photo** *of part of a lung was taken under a microscope, which magnifies it many times. The network of small passages inside the lung make it look and act rather like a sponge. An adult's lungs contain about 300 billion tiny blood vessels, called capillaries. If laid end to end, they would stretch over 1,200 miles (2,000 km).*

BREATH TEST

PROJECT

Fill a large plastic bottle and half-fill a large bowl with water.

Cover the bottletop with your finger and turn it upside down in the bowl. You will find that the water will stay in the bottle. Take a plastic tube and carefully put one end of it into the neck of the bottle, under the water. Now everything is ready for the breath test.

Blow hard into the free end of the tube. How much water can your breath push out of the bottle?

◗ **People who suffer from asthma,** *or other breathing difficulties, often use an inhaler to help them breathe. The inhaler puffs a drug down into the windpipe. This makes the air passages wider so they can breathe more easily.*

Making Sounds

We make sounds when we talk. We can whisper very quietly. We can laugh, scream, and sing. All the sounds that come out of our mouths are made in the throat.

Sounds are made by things vibrating, and your voice comes from vibrating vocal cords. These cords are soft flaps in the larynx, or voice box. They lie across the windpipe, behind the Adam's apple at the front of your throat.

To make loud sounds, we breathe hard over the vocal cords. If you put your hand on your throat and shout, you can feel the vocal cords vibrating.

When we cough, we release air at almost 60 mph (100 km/h), as we try to remove something that is irritating our airways.

◐ **We use our lips and tongue** *to change sounds from our vocal cords and form words. There are a thousand different languages in tropical Africa alone. This Masai man speaks one of them.*

VOCAL CORDS

closed

DO YOU SNORE?

You'll have to ask someone else for the answer to this question, unless you've ever woken yourself up by snoring very loudly. The noise is actually made by the soft part of the roof of the mouth vibrating. This can sometimes happen with such force that the loudest snores can make as much noise as a loud saw or even a pneumatic drill!

PROJECT

WHISTLING

When people whistle, they force air through a narrow opening at great speed. The air is squeezed so that it vibrates and makes a high-pitched sound called a whistle.

◆ **Our vocal cords** move to make sounds. Tiny muscles pull the cords together. They are specially designed to work and make sounds when air passes over them from below. But you can make them work when breathing in too. Try saying "hello" as you breathe in. It's like talking backward! When the cords are completely open, no sound is made.

open

◆ **Our lips and tongue** are controlled by hundreds of tiny muscles. These make them very flexible, so they can form words from the sounds made by the vocal cords. The difference in voices is due to the different sizes of the throat, nose, and mouth.

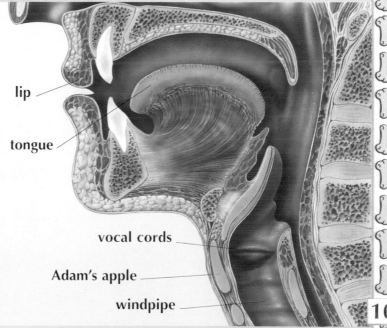

lip

tongue

vocal cords

Adam's apple

windpipe

Central Nervous System

brain

A network of nerves runs throughout your whole body. These nerves carry instructions from the brain, as well as messages from your sense organs back to the brain.

The nerves branch off from the spinal cord, which is connected to the brain. Together they make up the body's central nervous system. The brain is the body's control center. It tells the rest of the body what to do.

Our brain uses a huge amount of energy. It uses about a fifth of the oxygen we breathe, as well as a fifth of the energy in the food we eat. With this it produces electricity.

◐ **The brain is connected** to the spinal cord that runs down the body inside the backbone. Nerves run from the spine all over the body, even to your little toe.

spinal cord

nerve

❍ **Memories** are stored in the brain. This couple will always remember their wedding day.

MEMORY TESTER

PROJECT

Put a number of different objects on a tray or on the table. Choose different kinds of things. Then let a friend look at the objects for one minute. How many of the objects can your friend remember with her eyes closed? Now let her put a different set of objects on the table to test your memory.

◐ **If you tap** *the point below someone's knee, his or her leg will jerk. We call this a reflex action. Reflex actions help the body to protect itself quickly. They happen because the spinal cord sends a signal back to the muscle before the original message has reached the brain. In the same way, if you touch something hot, you pull your hand away in a reflex action.*

LEFT OR RIGHT?

The left half of the brain controls the right side of the body, while the right half looks after the left side. Very few people can write or draw well with both hands. Try using your "wrong" hand, to see how hard it is.

◐ **Our brain helps us** *to see and hear, as well as to judge speed and distance. A racing driver needs to do all these very quickly. His brain sends messages to his hands and feet to steer and control the car.*

Sleep

Sleeping takes up a lot of our time. Some people need more sleep than others, but most people spend about a third of their lives asleep.

We grow when we are asleep—so babies need at least 18 hours of sleep every day. Most children sleep for about 12 hours a night. As we grow less, we sleep less. Most adults sleep for between six and nine hours a night. Many old people need very little sleep.

Sleep gives the body time to rest. We often sleep more than usual

◑ Babies sleep *most of the time because their bodies are growing so quickly. If they don't get enough sleep, they cry and are unhappy. Young children need a lot of sleep too.*

◉ You may think *that you lie perfectly still at night, but you don't. People change their position many times during sleep. This is more restful for the body. If you stayed in one place all the time, your body would ache in the morning. We also breathe more slowly when we are asleep, and our hearts beat more slowly.*

◉ We often yawn *when we are tired and want to sleep. But what is it that makes us yawn? It could be that the body needs extra oxygen. A big yawn brings extra oxygen into the lungs. Yawning seems to be catching, but we do not know why. You may feel you want to yawn just looking at this picture!*

◆ **The brain** *makes a small amount of electricity, and this can be measured by sensors. The patterns are called brain waves, and they show scientists when we are dreaming. As we dream, the brain makes fast, regular waves, like it does when we are awake.*

when we are ill. We do this to give our body plenty of time to rest and mend itself. Our muscles have very little work to do when we are asleep, and so the parts of the brain that control movements can rest too. Our reflexes are still at work, however, so we might brush away a fly without realizing.

WHAT IS SLEEPWALKING?

Some people sleepwalk: they get up and walk around while they are asleep. They don't know they are doing it, and usually don't remember anything about it when they wake up.

◆ **Nightmares** *are scary dreams. Some people think that nightmares are useful, because they help the brain sort out our real fears and worries. A nightmare might be so scary that it wakes you up. Most people have bad dreams at some time.*

The Skin, Hair, and Nails

Skin protects the body and controls its temperature. It keeps out dirt, water, and germs, shields us from the Sun's rays, and stops the body drying out.

wavy hair

Our skin is full of nerve endings that send messages to the brain about things such as heat, cold, and pain. The skin produces nails to protect the tips of fingers and toes. It also grows hairs that provide extra warmth and protection.

nerve ending

epidermis

sweat gland

hair follicle

hair

dermis

blood vessel

◀ **The tough outer layer** of the skin is called the epidermis. It is waterproof and germproof. The inner layer, called the dermis, contains nerve endings. This is also where hairs grow and sweat is made.

106

straight hair

◐ **Hairs grow** *from follicles in the inner layer of our skin. Different-shaped follicles make people's hair straight, wavy, or curly.*

curly hair

◑ **People sweat** *when they are hot, so athletes sweat more on a very hot day. Sweat takes heat from the body and helps cool you down as it dries on your skin.*

half-
moon

nail

cuticle

fat

skin

bone

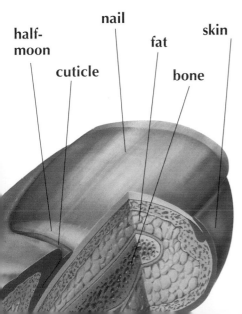

◖ **Nails** *are made of a tough substance called keratin. New nail grows from the base, under the skin. The pale half-moon is nail that has just grown.*

Teeth

Our teeth are there to break down food into small pieces, ready for swallowing. The teeth have three different shapes, designed to do different jobs.

The incisors at the front are for biting into food and cutting it up. The pointed canines tear tough food. And the big molars at the back grind and mash our food, which mixes with saliva and goes soft and mushy. This makes it much easier for us to swallow and digest.

If sugar and bacteria are left on the teeth for long, they can produce acid. This breaks down enamel and causes tooth decay. Regular brushing removes the sugar and bacteria.

⬥ **We should visit the dentist** *regularly to have our teeth checked and cleaned. Any tooth decay can be removed and replaced with a filling. When we are old, we may lose some teeth. The dentist can replace them with false teeth.*

CHECKING YOUR TEETH

PROJECT

Cleaning your teeth is important. Brushing helps to remove plaque, a filmy deposit on the surface of the teeth than can cause decay. Regular brushing every day means less plaque and so less tooth decay. It is sensible not to eat too much candy too. Clean teeth mean a healthy smile!

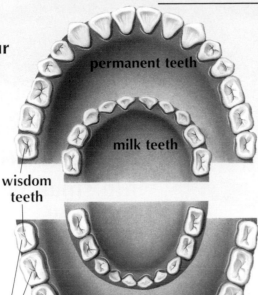

◖ **The four wisdom teeth** appear last, after the age of about 17. Some people never have wisdom teeth.

permanent teeth

milk teeth

wisdom teeth

molars

incisors

premolars

canine

◖ **As small children** we have 20 baby (or milk) teeth, shown in the inner circle. These start to fall out when we are 5 or 6 years old. The milk teeth are replaced by 32 permanent teeth, including four back wisdom teeth. It has been known for people to grow a third set of teeth, but this is very rare indeed.

◖ **It is important to look after your teeth** well when you are a child, so that they will be healthy and strong when you are older. Some children and young adults wear braces for a while. This helps to make crooked teeth straight.

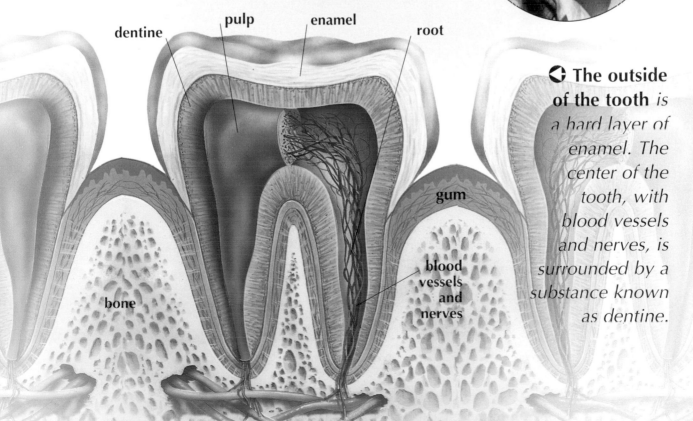

dentine

pulp

enamel

root

gum

blood vessels and nerves

bone

◖ **The outside of the tooth** is a hard layer of enamel. The center of the tooth, with blood vessels and nerves, is surrounded by a substance known as dentine.

Digestion

After we swallow food, it travels down a muscular tube to the stomach. There it is mashed into a souplike mixture.

The mixture passes into the small intestine, where tiny particles of food pass into the bloodstream. What's left of the food passes into the large intestine, and then waste products leave the body.

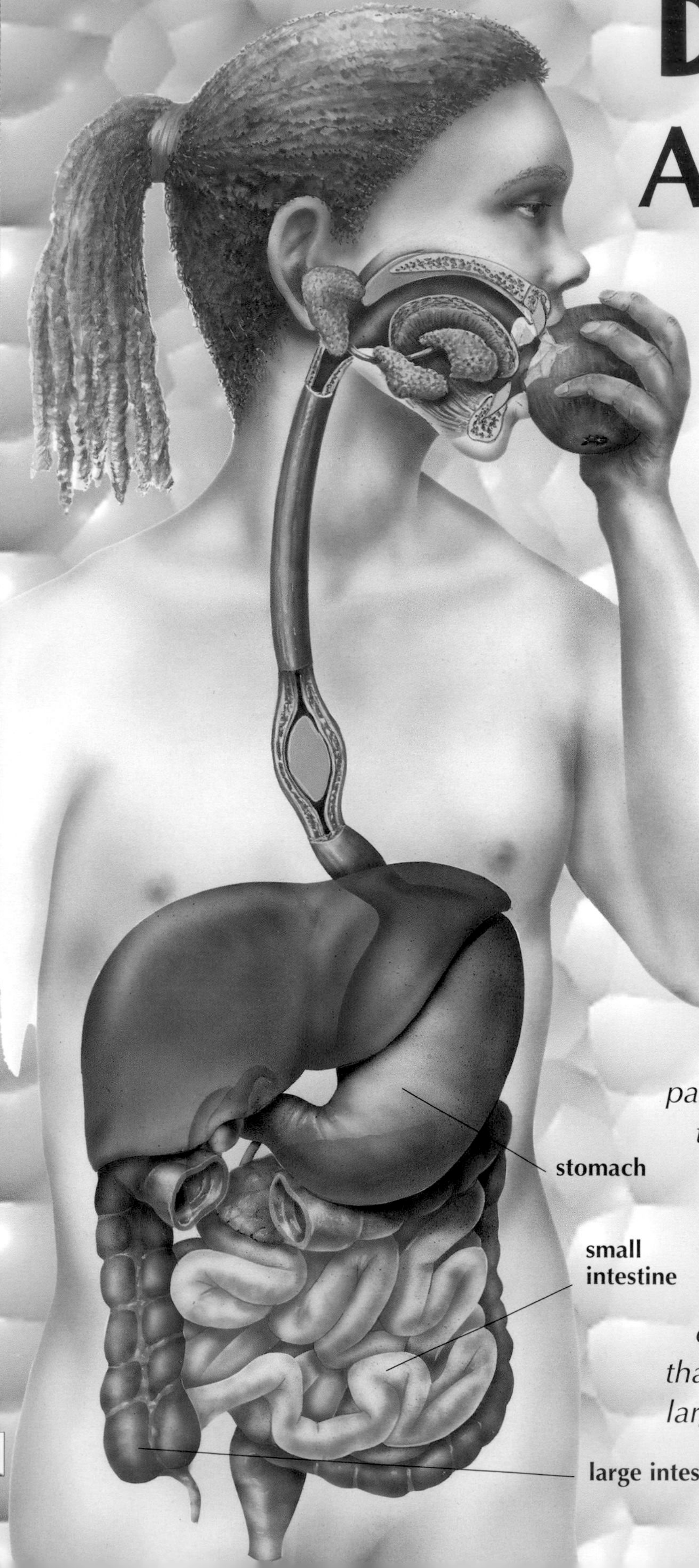

◆ **Digestion** *takes up to 18 hours, from biting the apple to tiny particles of it passing into the bloodstream. Food stays in the stomach for three hours. The small intestine is made up of over 16 feet (5 m) of coiled-up tube. It is longer than the large intestine, but the large intestine is much wider.*

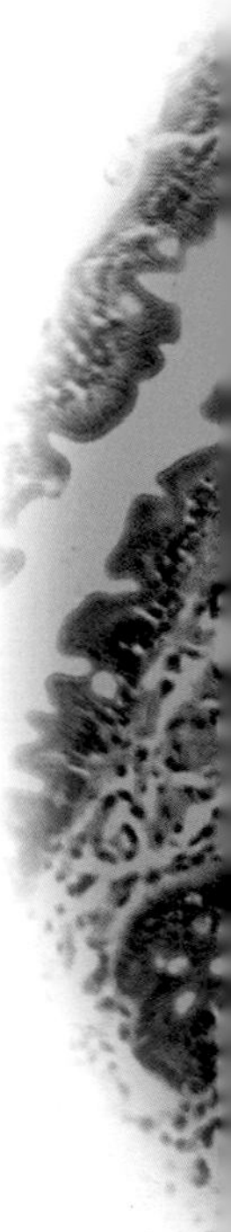

stomach

small intestine

large intestine

◄ **When we play,** *we use up a great deal of energy. We need to eat and digest food to provide our body with that energy.*

◆ **In the large intestine,** *water is taken out of the parts of food that our body cannot use. The water becomes urine and the rest is solid waste. These pass out of the body when we go to the toilet.*

◄ **Inside the small intestine** *are fingerlike bumps, called villi. These contain blood vessels that take the useful substances from food into our bloodstream. Blood, pumped by the heart, takes the energy from food to all parts of the body.*

Food and Drink

We need energy to live, and we get that energy from what we eat and drink. Our bodies need important substances, called nutrients, which we get from food. They help us grow and repair damaged cells, as well as providing energy.

◐ **Vegetables** *like these, and cereals such as wheat, are good to eat because they contain a lot of fiber. This helps other foods pass more easily through the digestive system.*

Different foods are useful to us in different ways. It is important that we don't miss out on any of the essential nutrients. To have a balanced diet, we must eat foods from various groups—carbohydrates, proteins, fats, and fiber.

◑ **Fruit and fruit juices** *such as orange juice contain a lot of Vitamin C, which keeps us healthy and helps us recover from illness. The body needs many other vitamins too.*

The body also needs small amounts of vitamins and minerals. Calcium (a mineral) is needed for healthy bones and teeth. Milk contains calcium, as well as water, fat, protein, and vitamins.

WHY DO WE NEED WATER?

The body uses water in many ways. Water helps to make up our blood. It keeps us cool by making sweat. It carries wastes from the body in urine. We get water from other drinks too, as well as from many different kinds of food.

◆ **Carbohydrates**, *such as bread and pasta, give us a lot of the energy that we need for our daily lives. We can make use of this type of energy very quickly.*

◆ **Beans and meat** *contain lots of proteins, which help us stay strong. Proteins are also used to make body cells, so they help us grow and stay healthy.*

PROJECT

HOME-MADE GRANOLA

Put 2 cups oats, 3/4 cup raisins, and 1/2 cup chopped nuts, along with some sunflower seeds, in a mixing bowl. Mix all the ingredients together. Then put your granola in a screw-top jar. Label the jar, adding the date. You can eat your granola with milk, yogurt, or fresh fruit juice, and have a healthy breakfast.

◆ **Fats** *such as cheese, butter, and milk are full of energy, as well as important vitamins. Fats can be stored by the body to use later, but it is not good to eat too many fatty foods.*

113

Smell and Taste

Smell and taste are important senses. Our sense of smell is much stronger than our sense of taste. When we taste food, we rely on its smell and texture to give us information about it as well.

We use our noses for smelling things. Tiny scent particles go into the nose with the air. The nose then sends messages through a nerve to the brain, which recognizes the smell. Most people can identify about 3,000 different smells.

The tongue also sends nerve signals to the brain about tastes. When we eat something, the tongue and the nose combine to let the brain know all about the food.

bitter

sour

salty

sweet

◆ **Nature makes nice and nasty smells!** *Flowers give off a pleasant scent that attracts insects, while a skunk can make a foul smell to scare off enemies.*

◆ **We taste different things** *on different parts of the tongue. We taste sweet things at the tip, salty things just behind the tip, sour things at the sides, and bitter things at the back of the tongue.*

WHY DO WE SNEEZE?

We sneeze to help clear our noses of unwanted particles, such as dust. When we sneeze, the explosive rush of air from the lungs can reach a speed of 100 mph (160 km/h)—as fast as a sports car!

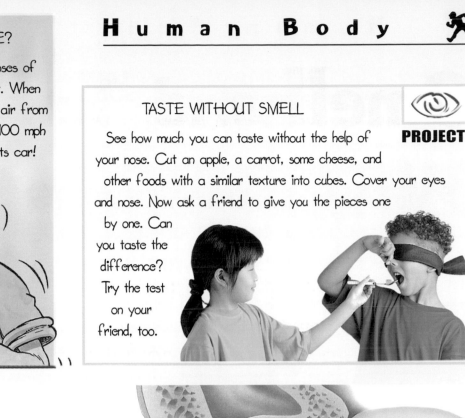

TASTE WITHOUT SMELL

PROJECT

See how much you can taste without the help of your nose. Cut an apple, a carrot, some cheese, and other foods with a similar texture into cubes. Cover your eyes and nose. Now ask a friend to give you the pieces one by one. Can you taste the difference? Try the test on your friend, too.

◆ At the top of the nose *are cells that are sensitive to scent particles. The particles dissolve in a lining of sticky mucus, and signals are sent along the olfactory nerve to a special part of the brain where smells are identified. When you have a cold and your nose is plugged, you lose the ability to smell things.*

olfactory nerve

scent-sensitive cells

mucus lining

◆ This photo of taste buds *was taken through a microscope. Our tongue has about 10,000 taste buds, which pick up the four basic tastes and pass the information on. Babies have taste buds all over their mouths, and also have a good sense of smell. As we grow older, our sense of smell gets weaker.*

Hearing

When we look at someone's ears, we see only a part of them. This part, called the outer ear, is shaped to collect sounds as they travel through the air.

All sounds are made by things vibrating. Sound waves make the eardrums and other parts vibrate. Information on vibrations is then sent to the brain, which lets us hear the sounds.

◖ **Sounds** *pass into the ear and make the eardrum vibrate, which in turn vibrates tiny bones. The bones shake a spiral tube, called the cochlea. Inside the cochlea is a fluid, which moves tiny hairs that send signals to the brain. Then we hear the sounds.*

outer ear

◑ **Good balance** *is very important to ballet dancers. Three canals next to the cochlea, in the inner ear, help us keep our balance. They let the brain know what movements the body is making.*

hammer   anvil   stirrup

🔽 **An old-fashioned ear trumpet** *works by acting as a bigger outer ear and making sounds louder. Modern hearing aids have tiny microphones and speakers.*

🔼 **Sounds travel well** *through liquids, so it is easy to hear when you are underwater. Whales and other sea creatures make sounds to communicate with each other.*

EARDRUM DRUM

PROJECT

To make a pretend eardrum, cut a large piece from a plastic bag. Stretch it over the top of a big can and hold it in place with a rubber band. Sprinkle sugar onto the plastic. Then hold a metal tray near to it and hit the tray with a wooden spoon. The grains of sugar will jump about as your drum vibrates with the sound.

ear
drum

stirrup

anvil

cochlea

hammer

◀ **A tiny bone** *called the hammer is connected to the eardrum. The eardrum vibrates the hammer. The hammer then moves the anvil, which in turn moves the stirrup bone. Finally, the stirrup vibrates the cochlea.*

Seeing

We use our eyes to see. Rays of light come into each eye through an opening in the middle called the pupil.

A lens inside each eye then bends the light very precisely, so that it travels to an area at the back of the eye called the retina. The light rays make an image on the retina, but the image is upside down. Nerves send information on the image to the brain, which lets us see it the right way up.

◗ **On a bright day,** *our eyes do not need to let in much light, so our pupils are small. At nighttime, when there is less light, they expand to let in as much light as possible. Small muscles change the size of the colored iris around the pupil.*

small pupil by day

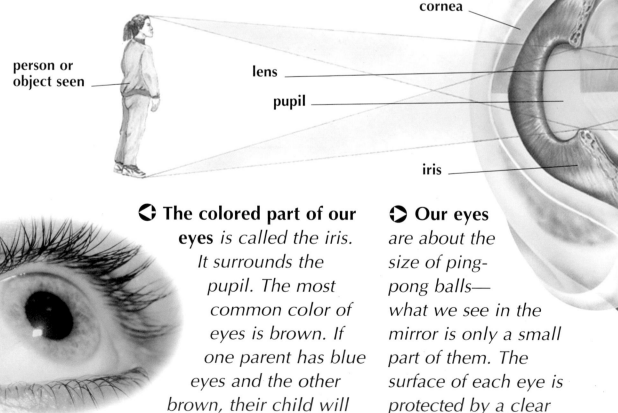

person or object seen

cornea

lens

pupil

iris

◖ **The colored part of our eyes** *is called the iris. It surrounds the pupil. The most common color of eyes is brown. If one parent has blue eyes and the other brown, their child will usually have brown eyes.*

◗ **Our eyes** *are about the size of ping-pong balls— what we see in the mirror is only a small part of them. The surface of each eye is protected by a clear shield called the cornea.*

large pupil at night

◗ *Most people see things in color, but about one in 12 men are colorblind—they find it difficult to tell the difference between some colors, especially red and green. This picture is a test for colorblindness. Can you see the shape inside the circle?*

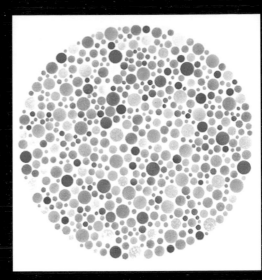

optic nerve

◗ **Many people** *wear glasses or contact lenses to help them see better. These change the direction of light before it enters the eyes, so that it focuses better on the retina.*

retina

WHY DO WE BLINK?

We blink about 15 times each minute, without thinking about it. The brain controls many actions such as this automatically. Blinking spreads tears across the eyes. This keeps the eyes clean and stops them from drying out. Tears keep the cornea at the front of the eye damp.

Touching

When we touch things, nerve endings just under the surface of the skin send messages to the brain through the central nervous system. The brain interprets the messages, and we feel things.

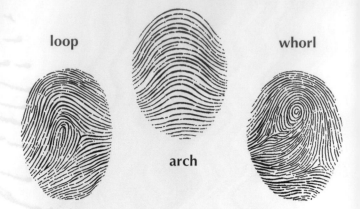

loop whorl

arch

🔵 **Every person's fingertips** *have a different skin pattern, called a fingerprint. These are the main fingerprint patterns.*

Our nerves can help us feel hardness, softness, and sharpness, for example. We can also feel heat and cold. Some parts of the body, such as our fingertips, have many more nerve endings than others. As well as our hands, the soles of our feet have many nerve endings. They have skin up to 1/8 inch (3 mm) thick, which is much thicker than on other parts of the body.

🔵 **Our sense of touch** *gives us information about the world. It allows us to learn about things around us without seeing them.*

Blind people *can read and write using a system called Braille. The letters of the Braille alphabet are a system of raised dots, which can be felt and understood through the fingertips. The Braille alphabet was invented by a Frenchman named Louis Braille (1809–1852). He went blind at the age of three, and later became an organ player and a professor.*

TOUCHY-FEELY GAME

PROJECT

Put lots of separate objects in a bag. Choose things that feel different, such as an apple, an orange, a soft toy, a brush, a stone, a pencil, and so on. Ask a friend to put one hand in the bag and guess what they can feel. Then ask your friend to put different things in the bag so you can have a turn at feeling and guessing.

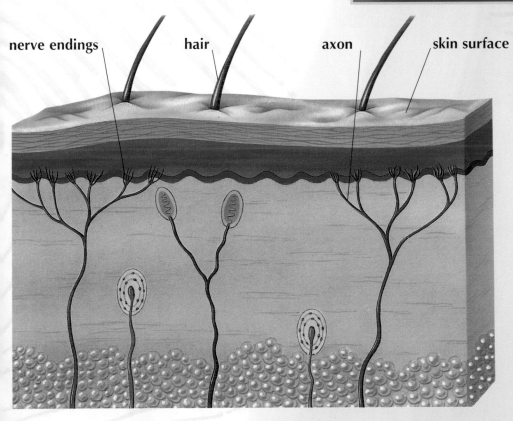

nerve endings | hair | axon | skin surface

Nerve endings *lie just beneath the surface of the skin. They send messages along threadlike axons. Nerve signals can travel through the body at 240 mph (400 km/h), so they reach the brain very quickly!*

How Babies Grow

Each of us began life as a tiny cell inside our mother's body. One of our father's sperm cells joined up with one of our mother's egg cells. The egg cell then began to grow, to make a baby.

Babies grow in the part of a woman's body called the womb. It takes about nine months for the cell to grow into a fully formed baby. As the baby gets bigger, the mother's womb stretches to make room for it. When it is ready, the mother's muscles start to push the baby out of her body and into the world.

sperm

egg

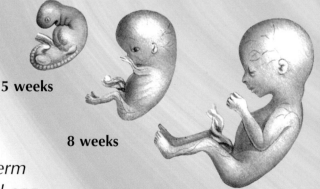

5 weeks

8 weeks

12 weeks

◆ **A man produces sperm.** *When one sperm joins up with a woman's egg, the fertilized egg starts to grow and develop into a baby.*

▶ **These are the organs** *that help a woman and a man make a baby. Eggs are made in a woman's ovaries. They move down the fallopian tubes next to the womb. Sperm is made in a man's testicles. It moves through tubes to the penis.*

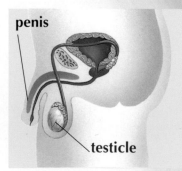

penis

testicle

fallopian tube

womb

vagina

ovary

❤ **Doctors can check** on a baby's health before it is born. They use a scanner that shows a picture of the inside of the mother's womb. They can even see whether the baby is a boy or a girl.

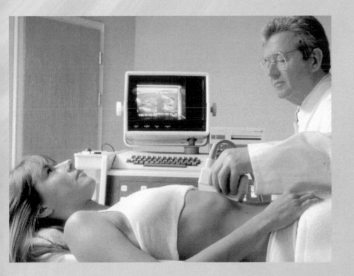

♦ **When children are born** to the same parents, they are brothers or sisters. Sometimes a mother has two babies at the same time, and these are called twins. They share the same birthday.

20 weeks　　30 weeks　　　　　　40 weeks

umbilical cord

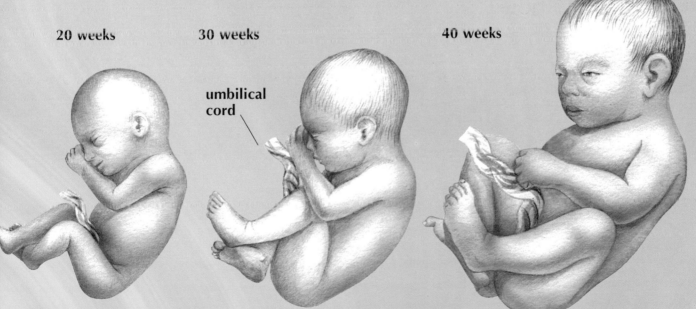

♦ **A baby grows** very quickly in a bag of warm liquid in the womb. It gets food and oxygen from its mother's body, through a tube called the umbilical cord. After eight weeks, it is about 1 3/4 inches (4 cm) long and has all its important body organs. By the time it is ready to be born, the baby is about 20 inches (50 cm) long. Immediately after being born, the baby's umbilical cord is cut. This leaves the baby with a mark on its stomach called the navel, or belly button.

Growing Up

Babies need a lot of love and care, because they cannot look after themselves. But babies grow and learn very quickly, so that, as young children, they can soon do a lot of things for themselves.

⬤ **Children love playing,** *and they learn a lot through play. When children play together, they learn about helping each other as well as about the objects and materials they play with.*

By the time a child is two years old, it is about half the height it will be as an adult. Young children go on growing quickly, reaching 75 percent of their adult height by the age of about nine. As teenagers, they have become young adults, and they start to make their own decisions and be independent. As adults, they generally leave their parents and eventually have children of their own.

◗ **A baby learns** *a huge amount in a short space of time. She learns to use her hands and feet to crawl and push herself up, before standing up and taking her first proper steps.*

124

HOW TALL?

The world's tallest person was Robert Wadlow (1918-1940). He was taller than most adults by the age of 10, and finally reached a height of 8 feet, 11 inches (2.72 m). That is over half as tall again as many grown-up people.

● **Most children enjoy** *going to school, where they make friends with other children and have fun. School helps to prepare children for adult life.*

● **When they have finished school** *or college, most people look for a job and start work. Some jobs, like a doctor, a lawyer, or a teacher for example, need special training and take many years to learn.*

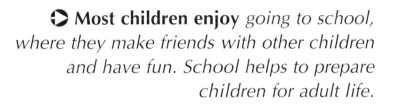

● **Older people** *usually retire from their jobs and spend more time on hobbies they enjoy, such as woodwork or gardening. More people today are living to be over 100. Jeanne Calment, who was born in France in 1875, died in 1997 at the amazing age of 122 years.*

Keeping Healthy

To stay healthy, we have to look after our bodies. We can make sure that we eat properly, get plenty of exercise, get as much sleep as we need, and keep ourselves clean.

Sometimes there is nothing you can do to stop yourself getting sick. But if you lead a healthy life, you will probably get better more quickly.

We can all avoid doing things that we know damage the body, such as smoking cigarettes, drinking too much alcohol, or taking harmful drugs. We can also be vaccinated against many diseases, either by injection or by mouth. Vaccination gives us a mild, harmless form of the disease, and stops us getting the disease later.

◑ **Sometimes we need to go to the hospital,** *where doctors and nurses help make us better. If you were to break a bone, you would need to go to a hospital for treatment.*

◑ **Many adults** *go to a gym or a sports club to have a workout and keep fit. Dance exercises can make you more supple.*

Flies and other animals *can spread germs and disease. That is why it is very important to store and serve food carefully, so that it stays fresh and is healthy for us to eat.*

Taking part in sport *is an enjoyable way to get lots of exercise. Exercise helps keep our muscles, as well as the heart and lungs, working well. It also helps keep bones strong. Swimming helps to make you strong and supple, and jogging is good for stamina. But if you are not used to exercise, don't suddenly do too much.*

⚠️ **WARNING**

Taking non-medical drugs is a sure way to damage your body and ruin your health. Never take anything that you think may be a drug or that you are not sure about.

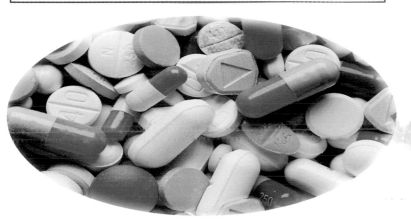

When we are ill, *the doctor may give us pills or medicine to help make us better. You must follow the doctor's instructions and never take pills without first asking for permission.*

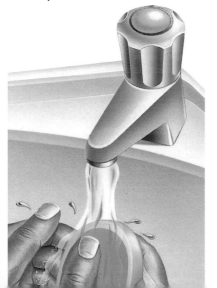

Washing with soap and water *helps keep us clean and gets rid of germs. You should always wash your hands after you have been to the toilet.*

127

Quiz

1. Which part of the body helps us to think and move? (page 90)

2. We are made up of billions of tiny living units – what are they called? (page 91)

3. What is the name of our framework of bones? (page 92)

4. Are you likely to be shorter or taller in the evening? (page 92)

5. Roughly how many muscles are there in the human body? (page 94)

6. Which muscle works together with the biceps? (page 95)

7. How many pints of blood does an adult body contain? (page 96)

8. Which blood vessels carry blood away from the heart? (page 97)

9. Does your heart beat faster or slower when you run? (page 98)

10. What do asthma sufferers use to help them breathe? (page 99)

11. What vibrate in your throat to make sounds? (page 100)

12. Why do we cough? (page 100)

13. Where is the spinal cord? (page 102)

14. Which half of the brain controls the left side of the body? (page 103)

15. How much sleep do babies need in a day? (page 10

16. What might you do when your body needs extra oxygen? (page 104)

17. Can different people have the same fingerprints? (page 106)

18. What are our nails made of? (page 107)

19. What are our pointed teeth called? (page 108)

20. What can you wear to make crooked teeth straight? (page 109)

21. Where does mixed-up food go after it leaves the stomach? (page 110)

22. What does the large intestine do? (page 111)

23. Why is fiber useful to us? (page 112)

24. What type of food are bread and pasta? (page 113)

25. Which part of the tongue tastes bitter things? (page 114)

26. Which nerve runs from the nose to the brain? (page 115)

27. Which bone does the hammer move? (page 117)

28. Can sound travel through liquids? (page 117)

29. What part of the eye bends light? (page 118)

30. In bright light, are our pupils big or small? (page 118

31. Where do nerve endings send messages? (page 120)

32. What is the alphabet system for blind people called? (page 121)

33. In which part of a mother's body does a baby grow? (page 122)

34. What is another word for belly button? (page 123)

35. Do babies learn quickly or slowly? (page 124)

36. How tall was the world's tallest person? (page 125)

37. What does vaccination do? (page 126)

38. What can help keep our muscles, heart, and lungs working well? (page 127)

Animals

The wildlife kingdom is full of all sorts of amazing animals—mammals, reptiles, birds, amphibians, fish, insects, mollusks, and crustaceans. They live in all parts of the world, in different habitats and with different life cycles and behavior. There is a lot to learn about them, and there are things we can learn from them.

Which mammals can fly? What is a marsupial? Where do penguins live? These and hundreds more questions have fascinating answers, telling us more about the creatures with which we share our planet. We can also learn to respect and look after those animals that are threatened by the way we live.

Mammals

There are many animals in the group we call mammals. A mammal has hair or fur on its body to keep it warm. Baby mammals are fed with milk from their mother's body.

Mammals live all over the world, from the freezing polar regions to the hot tropics. Most mammals live on land, but whales live in the sea and bats can fly. They are known as warm-blooded animals.

◆ **Kudu antelopes** *have beautifully curved horns. Males sometimes use these to fight each other. Kudus live in small groups in Africa, and their main enemies are leopards, lions, and wild dogs.*

◆ **Some mammals,** *such as this otter, have whiskers. These help them feel things and find their way about.*

◆ **The white rhinoceros** *is one of the world's five species of rhino. Hunters kill them for their horns, and rhinos are now rare in the wild.*

◆ **Bears** are large mammals with strong legs and big claws. Polar bears live in the freezing Arctic region. In midwinter, females dig dens in snowdrifts and give birth to their cubs there, protected from the cold and wind. The cubs stay in the den for about three months. Their mother feeds them with her own milk, though she eats nothing herself. In Spring she searches for food, such as seals.

◆ **Farm hogs** are descendants of wild boars. Farmers keep them for their meat—pork, ham, and bacon. All the piglets feed on their mother's milk at the same time.

The largest mammal is the blue whale. The largest on land is the African elephant. The tallest is the giraffe. The fastest is the cheetah. And the smallest is the tiny hog-nosed bat.

◆ **A porcupine** has long spines, called quills. It can raise and rattle its quills to warn off its enemies.

131

Apes and Monkeys

Apes are generally larger than monkeys, and have no tails. There are four types of ape. Gorillas and chimpanzees live only in Africa, and orangutans and gibbons live only in Southeast Asia.

Most apes and monkeys live in the world's rainforests or on grassy plains. They generally live together in large troops. Each troop has a leader, usually an old, strong male. They have good eyesight, hearing, and sense of smell.

◐ **Male mandrills** *have very colorful faces. Mandrills live in African forests, staying mainly on the ground in family groups. They feed on fruit, nuts, and small animals, and sleep in trees.*

◐ **Orangutans** *live in reserves in the tropical rainforests of Borneo and Sumatra. In the Malay language, this ape's name means "man of the forest."*

The New World monkeys of Central and South America, like this South American spider monkey, have very long tails, which they use to hold on to branches as they swing through the trees.

MONKEY MOBILE

PROJECT

Trace the monkey (right) and cut out its shape. Draw around the shape on cardboard and cut it out. Make two more monkeys and draw on faces. Make a small hole in each monkey and tie on pieces of thread. Tie the monkeys to some rolled cardboard and fix the knots with glue.

Chimpanzees are good with their hands. They use them to groom each other and pick off irritating pests. These humanlike apes also use sticks as tools to get honey from nests, and stones to crack open nuts.

The gorilla is the largest ape. Males are sometimes over 6 feet (1.8 m) tall—the same as a tall man. Gorillas are powerful, but they are also peaceful and gentle. They eat only plants.

133

Elephants

There are two species (or two kinds) of elephant—African and Asian. The African elephant is the world's biggest land animal. Males can grow up to 13 feet (4 m) high at the shoulder, which is over twice as tall as a man. They can weigh up to 7 tons, which is as much as 90 people!

Asian elephants are smaller and lighter, with smaller ears. They live in India, Sri Lanka, and parts of Southeast Asia.

◐ **Elephants love bathing.** *They can give themselves a shower by sucking water up into their trunks and spraying it over their bodies. When swimming across rivers, they sometimes use their trunks as snorkels, sticking them up out of the water so they can breathe in air.*

◑ **Asian elephants** *are used in the logging industry. They can lift and carry very heavy loads. A rider sits behind the animal's head and directs the elephant.*

DO ELEPHANTS USE SKIN CARE?

Yes! To prevent their skin from cracking, elephants wallow and cover themselves in cool mud. This dries on their bodies and helps protect them from the burning sunshine. It also gets rid of flies and ticks.

Female elephants live in family groups, which often join together to make large herds. Each group is led by the oldest female. She decides which routes the herd should take to find food and water. Adult male elephants usually live on their own.

◊ **Elephants** *have thick, wrinkled skin. Their eyesight is not very good, but they have good hearing and an excellent sense of smell. Their two long tusks, which are really big teeth made of ivory, are used for digging up roots and breaking off tree bark to eat. The trunk is used for plucking leaves and fruit.*

Cats

There are a number of species, or different kinds, of cats. Even the biggest wild cats are relatives of our pet cats at home!

All cats are meat-eaters. They are built to hunt, and their bodies are powerful. To help them catch their prey, cats have sharp eyesight and a good sense of smell. They can run very fast too. Their size, coloring, and coat patterns vary, but all cats have a similar shape.

⬥ **Cheetahs** *are the fastest cats. In fact, they are the fastest runners in the world. They can reach a speed of 60 mph (100 km/h) for a short distance.*

⬥ **Pet cats** *are used to living with people and being fed by their owners. But sometimes they hunt, chasing after birds and mice before pouncing.*

◐ Members of the cat family: *they look alike but live in different ways.*

jaguar

puma

lynx

black panther

leopard

◐ Tigers *are the biggest cats. From head to tail they measure up to 12 feet (3.6 m) long. These powerful animals make very good mothers to their baby cubs. Unlike pet cats and many of the big cats, tigers like water. They search out a pool during the hottest part of the day and cool off in the water. Tigers are excellent swimmers and can easily cross rivers.*

◐ Lions *are the only cats that live together in groups, called prides. Male lions have thick manes of hair. They lie around and let the female lionesses do most of the hunting. The strongest male may be challenged by other males, and have to fight to keep his rank as dominant male.*

WHY DO LEOPARDS HAVE SPOTS?

Because they make leopards difficult to see. The black spots on the yellow fur look like light shining through leaves. This is called camouflage. It helps the leopards hide from the animals they are hunting.

Whales and Dolphins

Whales and dolphins are mammals, not fish. Unlike fish, they cannot breathe underwater. So they come to the surface often, to take in air.

Whales and dolphins breathe in and out through a blowhole on the top of the head. When they let out used air, they usually send out a spray of water at the same time.

❂ The blue whale *is the largest animal in the world. It can grow up to 108 feet (33 m) long and weigh over 150 tons. Blue whales swim in all the world's oceans, usually alone or in small groups. Instead of teeth, blue whales have strips of whalebone, called baleen. When the whales take in water, the baleen traps tiny shrimps called krill.*

blue whale

◆ Common dolphins *can leap out of the water at great speed. Most dolphins swim at about 20 mph (30 km/h)—over three times faster than the quickest humans.*

◐ **The narwhal** *is a small Arctic whale with a long tusk, which is a spiral growth of the left tooth (it has only two teeth). Killer whales and sperm whales also have teeth, and dolphins are small toothed whales.*

WHALES TO SCALE

PROJECT

Draw whales and dolphins in scale with each other. You can use the scale 1:144. This means using an inch for every 12 feet, so your blue whale will be 9 inches long. The whales' real lengths are: common dolphin 6 feet, bottlenose dolphin 12 feet, narwhal 20 feet, pilot whale 25 feet, killer whale 30 feet, and the blue whale 108 feet.

◐ **Pilot whales,** *like the one at the top of the photo, have big, round heads. They live in large groups, called schools, of hundreds or even thousands. The other dolphin is a bottlenose.*

◐ **Some whales and dolphins** *are kept in zoos and dolphinariums. Killer whales are very popular performers. They can jump as high as 16 feet (5 m).*

Bats

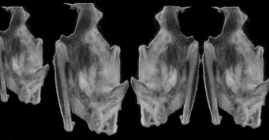

Bats are different from all other mammals in one way: they can fly. They do not have feathery wings like birds but, instead, have double layers of skin stretched over thin bones.

There are nearly a thousand different kinds of bats. Most are nocturnal, which means that they are active only at night. They sleep during the day and come out at night to find food. Most bats live on insects alone, but some eat fruit and nectar and others hunt small animals. Bats live in almost every part of the world, except the cold polar regions.

◆ **Bats hang upside down** *by their feet when they rest or sleep. They often live in caves, where there may be thousands of bats crowded together on the walls and ceiling. In a cave in Texas, 20 million free-tailed bats were found in one single colony!*

vampire bat

mouse-eared bat

● **Three different bat faces.** *The vampire bat lives in Central and South America. It uses its sharp teeth and tubelike tongue to suck animals' blood. A vampire bat's body is only about 4 inches (10 cm) long, but it has a wingspan of up to 7 inches (18 cm).*

◐ **Bats use echoes** *from their high-pitched squeaks to catch insects. The echoes help the bats make up a sound picture of what is around them. They do not need to use their eyes so much, but it is not true that they are "as blind as a bat."*

◑ **All bats** *have large, sensitive ears to steer by. These help them pick up echoes of the high-pitched sounds they make. Most bats have razor-sharp teeth.*

horseshoe bat

◐ **Bats are small creatures** *with large wings. A bat's long arm ends in four fingers and a strong, hook-shaped thumb. When its wings are folded, the bat can use its thumbs to climb trees or rocks.*

DO BATS FISH?

Some bats really do fish, in the same way that some birds do. The fisherman (or bulldog) bat of Mexico lives near mangrove swamps. When it hunts, it swoops down near the water. Then it dips quickly into the water with its clawlike feet, catches a small fish, and scoops it up into its mouth.

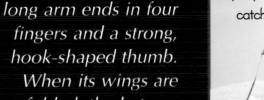

Marsupials

⬣ **The tiny honey possum** *feeds on pollen and nectar. Its 4 inch (10 cm) tail, which it uses for gripping like some monkeys, is longer than its body.*

Marsupials are a special group of mammals. Unlike all other animals, female marsupials have a pouch. They give birth to tiny babies, who stay in the pouch and live off their mother's milk until they are big enough to venture into the outside world. The soft pouch is warm and snug.

Most marsupials, such as kangaroos, koalas, and wombats, live in Australia. Some smaller kinds, called opossums, live in North and South America.

ROO RACERS

👁 **PROJECT**

Draw two kangaroos on cardboard and cut them out. Make a hole just below the head and run some string through. Tie one end of each length of string to a chair leg and lie the racers on their backs a couple of yards away. Then you and a friend can race your kangaroos by pulling on the string and then letting it go. The chair is the finishing line.

⬣ **Wallabies** *are like small kangaroos. They have long tails and long back legs, and move around in a series of hops, like kangaroos.*

◯ **Koalas** *are expert climbers. They spend most of their time in eucalyptus trees, eating the tender shoots. Although they look like small bears, koalas have nothing to do with the bear family.*

◯ **This female kangaroo** *has a joey in her pouch—a joey is what we call a baby kangaroo. Hopping on her huge back legs, she can travel more than 30 feet (9 m) in one leap.*

◯ **When a joey** *is big enough to leave the pouch, it jumps back in if there is danger, turns around, and pokes out its head.*

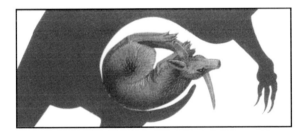

DO KANGAROOS BOX?

Sometimes male kangaroos, called bucks, try out their strength against each other. Standing on their hind (back) legs, they hit out with their arms, which looks like boxing. They also rest on their tails and kick out with their hind legs, which does more damage.

Reptiles

Snakes, lizards, and crocodiles are all reptiles. Unlike mammals, these scaly-skinned animals are all cold-blooded. This means that they always need lots of sunshine to warm them up.

◐ **Most reptiles lay eggs,** *which are soft and leathery. Snakes lay their eggs in shallow holes and cover them with soil. When the baby snakes hatch out, they have to look after themselves.*

Reptiles are found on land and in water. Most live in warm parts of the world, and some live in hot deserts. They move into a burrow if it is too hot above ground, or too cold in winter.

Most reptiles have four legs, but snakes are long, legless reptiles. All snakes are meat-eaters, and some kill their prey with poison from

◑ **The horned lizard** *has strong armor to protect it from its enemies. It has pointed scales, as well as horns behind its head. It lives in the dry areas and deserts of America, where it feeds mainly on ants. The female lays her eggs in a hole in the ground.*

◑ **Emerald tree boas** *live in the rainforests of South America. They wrap themselves around branches and watch out for prey, often birds and bats. They move fast and also swim very well.*

hollow teeth called fangs.

The longest snake is the reticulated python of Southeast Asia. It grows up to 30 feet (9 m) long. The largest lizard is the Komodo dragon of Komodo Island, Indonesia. It can grow up to 10 feet (3 m) long.

◑ **Chameleons** *are slow-moving, tree-dwelling lizards. If they see an insect within range, they shoot out a long, sticky tongue to catch it. They can also change color to suit their mood or their surroundings.*

◑ **Marine iguanas** *are the only lizards that swim in the sea. They live around the Galapagos Islands, in the Pacific Ocean. They go to sea to feed on seaweed, and then warm up on the rocks in the sunshine.*

Turtles and Crocodiles

Turtles and tortoises have a hard shell made of bony plates. Turtles move slowly on land but are good, fast swimmers. Tortoises, however, spend all their time on land.

Crocodiles and alligators belong to a group of reptiles called crocodilians. They are large, powerful animals with long tails and strong jaws. They live in or close to water and are found mainly in rivers in hot countries. During a long period of hot, dry weather, crocodiles may bury themselves deep in the mud and go to sleep. They will stay there until the weather changes.

◊ **Green turtles** *spend most of their time at sea, only coming on land to sleep and lay eggs. At nesting time they may travel thousands of miles to lay eggs on the beach where they were born.*

◊ **Hawksbill turtles** *are found near the rocky coasts and coral reefs of our oceans. Females lay about 150 eggs at a time.*

◐ **The gavial** *is a type of crocodilian with a long, thin snout. It has about 100 sharp teeth, which it uses to catch fish and frogs. Gavials can be found in the big rivers of Malaysia and northern India.*

◑ **Giant tortoises** *on the Galapagos Islands are huge. They weigh over 200 pounds (91 kg).*

◓ **American alligators** *live in the rivers and swamps of southeastern USA. The females are caring mothers. They carry their newly hatched babies in their mouths to a nearby pool. The young will grow to be more than 15 feet (4.5 m) long.*

MAKE A JUNK CROC

PROJECT

Crunch sheets of newspaper up into different-sized balls and arrange them into a crocodile shape. Make two jaws and four legs, and then tape everything together. Mix some wallpaper paste and stick thin strips of newspaper all over the crocodile with the paste. Stick on three layers, and then leave it to dry. Add some jagged cardboard teeth, two eyes, and paint the croc green all over.

Birds

Birds are the only animals with feathers. They have wings, and most are expert fliers. There are more than 9,000 different kinds, living in all parts of the world.

Female birds lay eggs, and most build nests to protect them. When the eggs hatch out, the adults feed their young until the small birds can fly and leave the nest.

DIFFERENT NESTS

osprey   ovenbird

◐ **Gulls** *and other seabirds glide over the sea, waiting to swoop down and catch fish. Many seabirds nest on rocky cliffs.*

◗ **Birds' beaks** *come in a variety of shapes for different uses. The macaw uses its hooked beak to crack nuts, a toucan grasps fruit in its long but very light bill, and an eagle tears flesh.*

Toucan

macaw

weaver bird

horned grebe

◆ **The Indian peacock** *spreads his tail feathers into a fan. He does this to attract the female peahen.*

North Pole

◐ **Arctic terns** *raise their young near the North Pole. Then they fly south to the Antarctic for the summer. In the fall they fly north again, making a round trip of 21,000 miles (36,000 km).*

South Pole

bald eagle

PROJECT

BIRD OF PARADISE

Draw a bird of paradise on blue cardboard with white crayon. Cut out pieces of colored paper to fit the head and body, and stick feather shapes on the body. Add long strips of tissue paper for the tail, and don't forget feet, a beak, and a button eye. You could make a rainforest background too, with real twigs and leaves.

Birds of Prey

Birds that hunt animals for food are called birds of prey. Eagles, hawks, and falcons all have hooked beaks and strong, sharp talons. They are fast fliers and have excellent long-distance eyesight. They can swoop down on their prey from a great height.

◀ **Owls** *have many advantages as night hunters. Their round faces help funnel sounds to their ear openings, which lie under feathered flaps. They can also turn their heads right around, to see behind them with their large eyes.*

Most owls hunt silently at night. Their feathers have a soft fringe that muffles the sound of their wings.

Vultures are scavengers. After an animal such as a lion has eaten its fill of a kill, the vultures gather to feed on the leftovers.

◼ **The peregrine falcon** *is the world's fastest bird. It can travel over 200 mph (350 km/h) as it dives toward its prey. It eats other birds, especially pigeons.*

◼ **White-backed vultures** *find plenty of food on the African grasslands. They wait for the big cats to have their meal first, then eat what is left. Afterward, they clean their feathers well, so that they are always in good flying condition.*

The world's biggest bird of prey is the condor of the Andes mountains in South America. Weighing up to 30 pounds, it can soar for long distances on its huge wings. It has a wingspan of 10 feet (3 m) and flies at up to 23,000 feet (7,000 m).

The bald eagle gets its name from its white head feathers. Bald eagles feed on fish, waterbirds, and rabbits. They live along coasts, rivers, and lakes in North America.

WHICH BIRDS USE TOOLS?

Egyptian vultures use stones as tools. They like to eat ostrich eggs, which are too big and tough to crack open with their beaks. So the vultures pick up stones and drop them on the eggs to crack them. Then they feed on the insides.

The osprey, or fish-hawk, is found in most parts of the world. An excellent catcher of fish, it circles over the water and then plunges in, feet forward, to snatch the fish in its talons. Sometimes the osprey dives right under the water to catch the fish.

Penguins

Like all birds, penguins are covered in feathers. The short, thick feathers are waterproof, and keep the animals warm in cold seas.

Penguins have a horny beak for catching food. They also have a small pair of wings, but cannot fly. They use their wings as flippers. These birds spend most of their time at sea and are fast, skilful swimmers.

There are 18 different kinds of penguin. They all live near the coasts of the cold southern oceans. Many live in the frozen region of Antarctica.

◐ **Antarctic emperor penguins** *keep their eggs and chicks on their feet, for warmth. While the male does this job, the female hunts for food in the sea.*

◓ **These Adélie penguins** *are waddling about on an ice floe off the coast of Antarctica. To climb out of the sea, penguins first dive down and then shoot out of the water at great speed, landing on their feet on the ice.*

emperor
penguin

little blue
penguin

○ **Penguins dive** *deep underwater, using their feet as rudders, to catch their food—mainly fish, squid, and small shrimplike krill. They come to the surface regularly to breathe. Gentoo penguins can swim at up to 16 mph (27 km/h).*

○ **The smallest penguins** *are "little blues," which stand 16 inches (40 cm) high. Emperor penguins are the biggest at 48 inches (120 cm) tall.*

○ **Rockhopper penguins** *have long yellow or orange feathers above their eyes. They often nest on clifftops, using pebbles or grass. They reach their colony by hopping from rock to rock, as their name suggests.*

A PENGUIN PLAYMATE

PROJECT

Pour sand into an empty plastic bottle and tape a washball to the top. Tape a cardboard beak to the head. Mix wallpaper paste and paste thin strips of newspaper over the penguin. When it's dry, paint the penguin white. Leave to dry again before painting the head, back, and flippers black, leaving white circles for the eyes. You could use your penguin as a bookend.

Amphibians

Frogs, toads, newts, and salamanders belong to a group of animals called amphibians. They spend part of their lives on land and part in water, but amphibians don't live in the sea.

Amphibians go back to water when it is time to lay their eggs. Females may lay their eggs in or near a pond or stream. Most frogs and toads lay between 1,000 and 20,000 eggs in large clusters, called spawn.

Toads usually have a rougher skin than frogs. It is often covered with warts.

🔺 **Tree frogs** *have round suckers at the ends of their toes. These help them to grip trunks, branches, and even shiny leaves.*

⬟ **Arrow-poison frogs** *of South America are very poisonous. Females lay up to six eggs on land. When they hatch, the male carries the tadpoles on his back to a tree hole filled with water or to a water plant, so that they can begin life in water.*

FROG LIFE CYCLE

A frog's eggs hatch into tadpoles in the water. The tadpoles grow legs and turn into froglets. Finally the young frogs can leave the water and hop out onto land.

Frogs *have long back legs. These are good for swimming—we copy their action when we swim breaststroke. The powerful legs are also useful for jumping on land. Common frogs can leap about 2 feet (60 cm), and South African sharp-nosed frogs can jump over 10 feet (3 m)!*

WHAT ARE MOUTH-BROODERS?

A male mouth-brooding frog can gather up to 15 eggs with its tongue and put them in its mouth. But it doesn't eat the eggs. It keeps them in its vocal sac, where they turn into tadpoles. When the froglets are ready, they jump out.

Toads usually live in drier places. They have wider bodies and shorter, less powerful legs, which means they are not such good jumpers. Female Surinam toads keep their eggs in holes in their skin, where the young toads develop.

This smooth-skinned giant salamander *lives in the rivers, lakes, and cool, damp forests of western USA. It can grow to 12 inches (30 cm) long. Most salamanders are silent, but this one can make a low-pitched cry.*

swimming tadpole

froglet with legs

young frog

frog's eggs or spawn

Fish

There are more than 20,000 different kinds of fish in the world's oceans, lakes, and rivers. Like other animals, fish live in warm parts of the world, as well as in cold polar seas.

Many fish have streamlined bodies and fins to help them swim. They have gills instead of lungs, so that they can breathe under water. Fish have the same body temperature as the waters in which they live and swim.

⚫ **The long, thin trumpet fish** *grows up to 3 feet (nearly 1 m) long. Its eyes are set well back from its jaws. Compare its shape to the ray and the porcupine fish.*

⚫ **Seahorses** *look very strange. They swim in an upright position and live near seaweed, which they can hold on to with their tails. Seahorses are fishes that can change color.*

⚫ **A giant manta ray** *feeds on tiny sea creatures as it swims through the ocean. Rays have flat bodies, and most rays swim close to the sea floor or lie hidden on the bottom.*

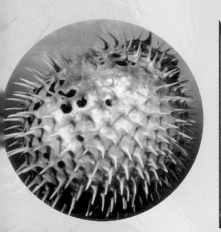

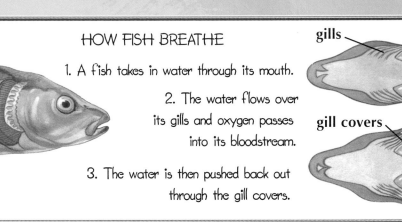

HOW FISH BREATHE

1. A fish takes in water through its mouth.

2. The water flows over its gills and oxygen passes into its bloodstream.

3. The water is then pushed back out through the gill covers.

gills

gill covers

This porcupine fish can swell up into a spiny ball. No enemy would risk eating such a prickly mouthful.

The lionfish has fins sticking out all over its body, and a row of poisonous spines. It can grow up to 15 inches (38 cm) long.

Moray eels swim with their mouths open, ready to catch smaller fish. Their relatives, the electric eels of South America, kill fish with electric shocks from their tail. They grow up to 6 feet (1.8 m) long.

The butterfly fish is brightly colored and has strong contrasting markings on its sides.

Sharks

Sharks are the fierce hunters of the world's oceans. People are very frightened of them, though many sharks are quite harmless.

Most fish have an air bag, called a swim bladder, which helps to keep them afloat. Sharks don't have a swim bladder, which means they have to keep swimming all the time, or else they would sink to the bottom. Sharks are different from most other fish in another way too. A shark's skeleton is made of rubbery cartilage instead of bone.

◑ **Tiger sharks** *are thought to be dangerous to people, but any shark will only attack if it smells blood. All sharks have an excellent sense of smell and good hearing, helping them hunt at night.*

The harmless whale shark is the world's largest fish, growing over 40 feet (12 m) long. It uses its huge mouth as a scoop for catching tiny sea creatures. The smallest shark is the dwarf shark, at just 6 inches (15 cm) long.

◑ **Shark's teeth** *form double or triple rows and are set inside a tooth bed. New teeth are formed in grooves in this area every 1–2 weeks to replace old or worn-out teeth.*

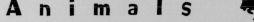

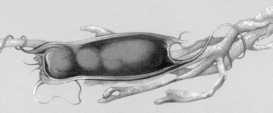

⬥ **Some sharks lay eggs** *rather than giving birth to live babies. They lay their eggs in a tough case, called a mermaid's purse, which attaches itself to weeds. The baby fish grow inside the case.*

⬥ **Reef sharks** *live near coral reefs, where there are plenty of smaller fish and other sea creatures for them to feed on.*

⬥ **A metal cage** *protects divers from big, inquisitive sharks. The great white shark, seen here with jaws gaping to grab bait, can grow to 20 feet (6 m) or more long.*

⬥ **The great white shark** *is the most famous of all the sharks. It grows up to 20 feet (6 m) or more long.*

Insects

Insects are tiny animals that are found all over the world—from scorching deserts to steaming rainforests and icy lakes.

Insects have no backbone. They are protected by a hard, outer skeleton or shell. Because they are so small, they can fit into tiny places and don't need much food to live on. They all have six legs, and most have wings and can fly. Many insects have two pairs of wings, but flies have just one pair.

antennae

head

thorax

abdomen

◑ **This wasp** shows the three basic body parts of an insect—a head, a thorax, and an abdomen. Its legs and wings are attached to the thorax, and its antennae to the head.

◑ **Beetles** *live just about everywhere on Earth. Some live in water, and many can fly. This horned beetle is found in Borneo, in Southeast Asia.*

◑ **Ladybugs** *are a kind of beetle. They feed on tiny insects called aphids, which they find on plants. The ladybug's hard, outer wings protect the flying wings, which lie underneath.*

ZIGZAG LADYBUG

PROJECT

Fold a large piece of paper backward and forward into a zigzag. Then draw a ladybug shape at one end, making sure that a part of the ladybug's body joins each edge. Cut out the ladybug, but don't cut the zigzag edges. Unfold the paper and color in all your ladybugs. You could make a chain of buzzing bees too.

Termites *live in colonies and build huge mounds as nests. Each colony is ruled by a king and a queen. Soldier termites defend the nest. Most of the termites are workers.*

termite mound

tunnel

queen's chamber

egg chamber

food store

WHY DO WASPS STING?

Wasps mainly sting to defend themselves and their nests. They also use their sting to stun or kill other insects. The sting is really a tiny tube. When it is hooked in place, the insect pumps poison down the tube.

This honey bee *is collecting nectar and pollen from a flower. The bee will take the food to its nest, where it will be stored as honey. A single bee would have to visit more than 4,000 flowers to make one tablespoon of honey. A large beehive may contain 60,000 worker bees.*

Female mosquitoes *are bloodsuckers. They insert a needlelike tube into birds and mammals, including humans, and suck up a tiny amount of blood.*

Butterflies and moths

🔺 **This peacock butterfly** *has eyespots on its wings. The spots may confuse or scare a hungry bird, which sees what look like the eyes of a bigger animal. The butterfly escapes being eaten.*

Butterflies have thin, delicate wings, covered with tiny overlapping scales. These give butterflies their wonderful colors.

Like many insects, butterflies change their bodies as they develop. This change is called metamorphosis. Eggs develop into caterpillars. Each caterpillar turns into a chrysalis, and the final stage is a beautiful, brightly colored butterfly. The largest known butterfly in the world is the

🔺 **A hawkmoth caterpillar.** *In other insects, this stage is called a larva. We call small insect larvae grubs or maggots. Hawkmoths (above right) feed on nectar, which they drink from flowers through their long, tube-shaped tongues. They have large bodies and are fast fliers.*

👁️ BUTTERFLY PRINTS

PROJECT Fold a sheet of paper in half. Open it up and drop blobs of different-colored paints around the crease in the middle of the paper. Fold the two halves over and press the paper down. When you open it again, you will see that you have made a beautiful butterfly. When they are dry, cut your butterflies out and hang them up.

◆ Male and female butterflies *are often very different. This is a male Adonis blue butterfly. The female's wings are brown.*

Queen Alexandra's birdwing, with a wingspan of more than 11 inches (28 cm).

Moths are night-fliers and usually have much duller colors than butterflies. At rest, their wings lie flat rather than folded up.

◆ A caterpillar *hatches from a butterfly egg. The caterpillar becomes a pupa, or chrysalis. A butterfly develops inside the pupa, and eventually emerges.*

caterpillar

egg

pupa

butterfly

◆ Butterflies *have a very keen sense of smell. They mainly use their antennae to smell, but some smell through "noses" on their feet!*

◆ Unlike most moths, *the emperor moth flies by day. Females give off a strong scent, which males can pick up half a mile away.*

Spiders

Spiders are similar in some ways to insects, but they belong to a different group of animals called arachnids. Scorpions, ticks, and mites are arachnids too.

Spiders have eight legs, while insects have six. Many spiders spin silky webs to catch flies and other small insects. They have fangs for seizing their prey. Most spiders paralyze their prey with poison before they kill and eat them. But only a few spiders are poisonous to humans.

◆ **Most spiders** *and other arachnids have eight eyes. But spiders still do not see very well. They rely on touching things to know what is going on around them.*

◆ **A jumping spider** *has big eyes, all the better to spot its next meal. Some spiders have eight eyes, others only two or none at all.*

◆ **Trapdoor spiders** *have a very clever system for catching insects. The spider digs a burrow, lines it with silk, and covers the entrance with a trapdoor. Then it lies in wait. When an insect passes nearby, the spider feels the ground move. It jumps out and catches the insect, quickly dragging it into its burrow.*

There are about 40,000 different kinds of spider, and there can be many millions of each type. In a grassy meadow, there may be as many as 50 spiders in a square foot.

Female spiders lay up to 2,000 eggs, which they wrap in a bundle of silk threads. Spiderlings hatch from the eggs.

Garden spiders spin beautiful circular webs. When an insect is caught in a web, the spider feels the silk threads of the web move. Then it rushes out and ties up its prey in a band of silk. The webs are easily damaged, and the spiders spend a lot of time repairing them. We can see webs best when the air outside is damp.

Mollusks and Crustaceans

Some mollusks, such as octopuses, have soft bodies. Others, such as snails, are protected by shells. Some mollusks live on land, but many live in the sea.

Crustaceans get their name from their crusty covering. Most of them, such as crabs, lobsters, and shrimp, live in the sea. A few crustaceans, such as woodlice, live on land.

◑ **Octopuses** are eight-armed mollusks. Many are very small, but the largest have tentacles up to 12 feet (3.5 m) long. Octopuses can change color according to their surroundings, so they can easily hide.

◐ **A garden snail's soft body** has a muscular foot, which it uses to creep along. The snail's whole body can be pulled safely into its shell if it is threatened by another animal.

Mollusks and crustaceans all begin life as eggs, and most of them have a larva stage.

The world's largest crustacean is the giant spider crab, which has a legspan of almost 13 feet (4 m)!

◆ Sallylightfoot crabs *live on the rocky shores of the Galapagos Islands, off South America. As they grow, they shed their shells and grow bigger ones. They measure up to 6 inches (15 cm) across. Crabs' legs are made in such a way that they can walk sideways. The front pair of legs has strong pincers for picking up food.*

◆ Lobsters *are among the largest crustaceans. They walk across the seabed on four pairs of legs.*

◑ Hermit crabs *use the shells of sea snails for protection. Some kill and eat the snail to get both a meal and a home. When it outgrows the shell, the crab looks for a new one.*

◁ Squids *are related to octopuses. They take in water and push it out again through a funnel behind their heads. This shoots them along backward.*

CAN SQUIDS SHOOT INK?

Squids and octopuses can shoot out a stream of inky fluid when they want to get away from enemies. The ink clouds the water and confuses the enemy, giving the mollusk time to escape.

Quiz

1. What do baby mammals feed on? (page 130)

2. Where do polar bears give birth? (page 131)

3. Can you name four kinds of apes? (page 132)

4. Where do orangutans live? (page 132)

5. Which is the world's biggest land animal? (page 134)

6. What do elephants eat? (page 135)

7. Which are the fastest cats? (page 136)

8. Which big cat likes water? (page 137)

9. How long is a blue whale? (page 138)

10. What does a narwhal have on its head? (page 139)

11. What is different about bats, compared with other mammals? (page 140)

12. What do bats use to catch insects? (page 141)

13. What are baby kangaroos called? (page 143)

14. Which trees do koalas live in? (page 143)

15. Are reptiles warm-blooded or cold-blooded? (page 144)

16. Where do emerald tree boas live? (page 144)

17. What is the difference between turtles and tortoises? (page 146)

18. Where do giant tortoises live? (page 147)

19. What is a female peacock called? (page 149)

20. Which bird takes its name from its beautiful woven nest? (page 149)

21. What do we call birds that hunt animals for food? (page 150)

22. Which is the fastest bird? (page 150)

23. What do penguins eat? (page 153)

24. Which are the largest and the smallest penguins? (page 153)

25. How do tree frogs grip branches? (page 154)

26. What is one of the main differences between frogs and toads? (page 154)

27. What do fish use to breathe? (page 157)

28. How do electric eels catch their prey? (page 157)

29. What happens to sharks if they stop swimming? (page 158)

30. Which is the world's smallest shark? (page 158)

31. What are the three main parts of an insect's body? (page 160)

32. What kind of insect is a ladybug? (page 160)

33. In the life cycle of a butterfly, which stage comes after the caterpillar? (page 162)

34. How are butterflies and moths different when they rest? (page 163)

35. How many legs does a spider have? (page 164)

36. How do garden spiders catch insects? (page 165)

37. Which crab steals its home from other sea creatures? (page 167)

38. Is it true that crabs can walk sideways? (page 167)

Long Long Ago

The story of life on Earth takes us right back to the early days of our planet. In recent times we have learned a great deal about life's history, including the fascinating period that we call the Age of Dinosaurs.

For many millions of years, the land was dominated by meat-eating and plant-eating dinosaurs, while plesiosaurs swam in the oceans and pterosaurs flew in the skies. Then all these reptiles, many of them giants, died out. They were replaced by mammals, who gradually came to dominate the planet. Through our study of fossils, we can now piece together how this all came about.

Early Life

Life on Earth has been developing and changing over billions of years. Scientists now believe that the simplest forms of life began in the world's oceans, probably over three billion years ago.

We can only guess what the very first plants and animals looked like. But we think that many early sea animals had soft bodies, without shells, bones, or other hard parts. They included jellyfish, different kinds of worms, and other creatures related to starfish. The first fishes had a head, a backbone, and a tail, but no fins or jaws. They sucked food into their mouths instead of biting it.

◖ **Fast-moving, armor-plated fish** *like this Coccosteus ruled the seas about 370 million years ago. It was about 16 inches (40 cm) long, and had sharp bony ridges and tusks inside its strong jaws. It could easily catch and eat slower-moving shellfish.*

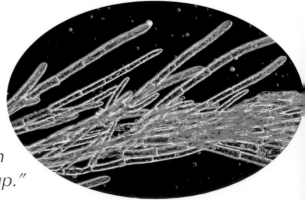

◗ **This is blue-green algae,** *one of the simplest forms of life, seen through a microscope. It is made up of a skin surrounding only a watery "soup."*

Shallow coastal areas of the early oceans were full of red, green, and brown algae, or seaweeds. Today, there are about 7,000 different kinds of seaweed.

These jellyfish, sea pens, and worms lived in the oceans about 650 million years ago. They were animals without backbones.

Scientists thought that Coelacanths died out about 70 million years ago. But in 1938, a fisherman caught one in the Indian Ocean. These ancient fish grow up to 6 feet (2 m) long.

HOW OLD ARE SHARKS?

The ancestors of today's sharks were swimming in the seas about 400 million years ago. They are one of the oldest animal groups with backbones still alive today.

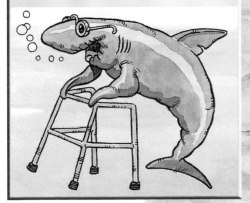

Evolution

Most scientists believe that different forms of life on Earth developed and changed very slowly over millions of years. They call this gradual process "evolution."

Animals and plants have evolved with time, as one generation followed another. Tiny changes in one generation amounted to big changes over millions of years.

◐ **In 1832, scientist Charles Darwin** *(1809–1882) arrived in South America. There he found fossils of extinct animals. His studies of these and living animals led him to develop his famous theory of evolution.*

As the world changed, it suited some animals better than others. Those animals which adapted easily to their surroundings did well and became more plentiful, while others died out over time.

◆ **The horse** *has developed over 50 million years. The first horse, Hyracotherium, lived in swampy forests and was as big as a modern fox. The modern horse, Equus, appeared about 3 million years ago.*

Hyracotherium, the first horse

Mesohippus

Merychippus

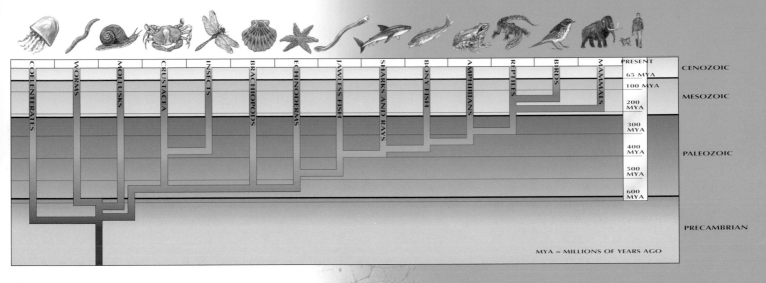

															PRESENT	CENOZOIC
COELENTERATES	WORMS	MOLLUSKS	CRUSTACEA	INSECTS	BRACHIOPODS	ECHINODERMS	JAWLESS FISH	SHARKS AND RAYS	BONY FISH	AMPHIBIANS	REPTILES	BIRDS	MAMMALS		65 MYA	
															100 MYA	MESOZOIC
															200 MYA	
															300 MYA	
															400 MYA	PALEOZOIC
															500 MYA	
															600 MYA	
																PRECAMBRIAN

MYA = MILLIONS OF YEARS AGO

◐ **This chart** *shows how life has developed over millions of years. Human beings appeared not so long ago.*

◑ **Giraffes** *developed very long necks and legs so that they could feed from leaves on the highest branches, where other creatures could not reach.*

Equus, modern horse

Pliohippus

The Age of Amphibians

swampy forest

peat bog

About 360 million years ago, some sea creatures left the water and crawled out onto land. Already there were many different fish in the sea, as well as plants and insects on land.

By now some animals could live on land and in water. We call these animals amphibians, which means "having a double life." Steamy swamps and forests were an ideal place for them to live. Amphibians laid their eggs in water. The eggs hatched into swimming tadpoles, and when the tadpoles became adults, they moved onto the land. This is exactly how amphibians such as frogs and toads live today.

Early amphibians were much bigger than today's amphibians. The early giants died out about 200 million years ago. But there is one exception, a giant salamander that lives in China and grows to a length of 6 feet (1.8 m).

⊃ **Ichthyostega** *was one of the first amphibians. It was about 3 feet (1 m) long. Giant dragonflies and other insects lived among the tall ferns.*

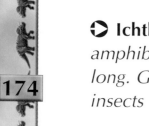

coal

rocks

Dead leaves and branches formed layers of plant material in the swampy forests of the early amphibians. This made peat, and when peat was covered by rocks, the pressure turned it into coal.

Some leaves survived intact as ancient coal formed, and made fossils like this one. These have provided us with knowledge about the past.

This North American bullfrog is a good example of a modern amphibian. Bullfrogs spend most of their time near water. All frogs breathe through lungs, as well as through their skin. Today there are about 4,000 different kinds of amphibians, including frogs, toads, newts, and salamanders.

Ichthyostega

175

Early Reptiles

About 300 million years ago, in the world's swampy forests, the first reptiles appeared (the name "reptile" comes from the Latin word for "crawl").

Reptiles were small, lizard-like animals that fed mainly on insects and worms. By 280 million years ago, the amphibians were becoming less common and there were many different kinds and sizes of reptiles.

Reptiles were different from amphibians in one important way: they could live on land all the time. They didn't need to lay their eggs in water. The eggs were protected by a leathery shell, and had their own supply of food and water inside. The young reptiles hatched out as tiny versions of their parents. This was unlike the way in which amphibians developed. Reptiles became the world's first true land dwellers.

◁ **Dimetrodon** *was a large sail-backed reptile that grew to over 12 feet (3.6 m) long. The reptile's skeleton shows how the huge sail, or fin, on its back was supported by long spikes growing out of its backbone.*

◐ **Mesosaurs** *were reptiles that found food in the sea. They caught fish with their needlelike teeth, which interlocked when they closed their jaws.*

◐ **Some reptiles** *developed "sails" on their backs. These absorbed the Sun's heat, helping the reptiles to warm up quickly. If the creatures got too hot, the sails gave off heat like a radiator, letting them cool down.*

WHICH WERE THE RULING REPTILES?

The archosaurs, or "ruling reptiles," developed after the early reptiles. Some looked like crocodiles. Others walked on their back legs, like the later dinosaurs.

◑ **Lycaenops** *was an extremely fierce, fast-moving reptile that attacked and killed plant-eating reptiles and slower-moving amphibians. It lived about 230 million years ago.*

Over millions of years, many sorts of scaly-skinned reptiles evolved, both large and small. Some ate plants and some fed on other animals. At first they had legs at the sides of their bodies. Later some had legs that were more underneath, which meant they could run faster.

Dinosaurs

The Age of the Dinosaurs is divided into three periods: the Triassic (240–205 million years ago), the Jurassic (205–138 million years ago), and the Cretaceous (138–65 million years ago). The first dinosaurs appeared on Earth about 230 million years ago, in the Triassic.

◊ **Hundreds of dinosaur skeletons** *have been found in the badlands of Dinosaur Provincial Park, in Alberta, Canada. Rain and snow have worn away the rocks, uncovering the reptile remains. Dinosaur collectors first rushed to the area in the early 1900s.*

The name dinosaur means "terrible lizard," but these reptiles were only distantly related to lizards and most of them were not terrible! For 165 million years, they dominated the land. Some dinosaurs were huge, others were quite small. Some were meat-eaters, others ate only plants. They lived everywhere on Earth.

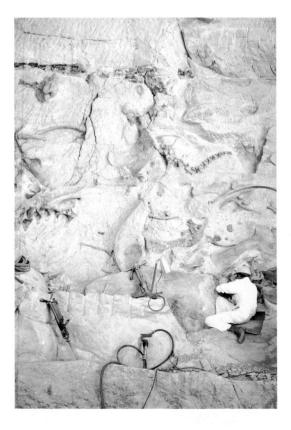

◊ **This scientist** *is working at Dinosaur National Monument, Utah. More than 5,000 dinosaur fossils have been found there. The most common remains have been those of Stegosaurus. Large bones are taken by helicopter or truck to museums, where scientists put the pieces together for display.*

There are two main groups of dinosaurs—lizard hipped and bird hipped. *All the meat-eating dinosaurs, including Tyrannosaurus (big skeleton shown), and the big four-legged plant-eaters had hips shaped like those of a modern lizard. The other group, which included Stegosaurus (smaller skeleton shown), had hips like a bird. Bird-hipped dinosaurs evolved later and were all plant-eaters.*

The plant-eating Ultrasaurus, *a huge sauropod, was the largest land animal ever to live. It was about 100 feet (30 m) long. With its long neck, it was tall enough to look over a modern three-storey house.*

SIZES

Dinosaurs came in all sizes. Compsognathus was a small, fast-moving meat-eater with very sharp teeth. It was 28–56 inches (70–140 cm) long, including its long tail. It probably ate large insects, lizards, and small mouselike mammals.

Brontosaurus *was renamed Apatosaurus as it was the same as the earlier fossil.*

Meat-eating Dinosaurs

The dinosaur carnivores, or meat-eaters, were powerfully built animals. They walked upright on their two back legs, and their shorter arms ended in hands with clawed fingers.

◆ **Baryonyx** *had long, curved thumb-claws (above left). Tyrannosaurus had enormous teeth (above right). They were up to 7 inches (18 cm) long, with sharp edges like steak knives. Tooth finds help tell us what dinosaurs fed on.*

Big meat-eaters such as Tyrannosaurus had huge heads on short necks. They had very strong, sharp teeth. Nearly all meat-eaters had long, muscular tails, which they carried straight out behind them. This helped them to

◆ **Tyrannosaurus** *was about 40 feet (12 m) long and weighed over 6 tons. Its forward-facing eyes helped it to judge distance well as it moved in to attack smaller dinosaurs.*

balance their heavy weight. Their strong back legs made meat-eaters the fastest of all the dinosaurs.

❖ **Allosaurus** *was one of the biggest meat-eaters before Tyrannosaurus. It was 36 feet (11 m) long. We don't know what color dinosaurs were, but some may have been brightly colored.*

WHICH WAS FASTEST?

We don't know how fast dinosaurs could run, but scientists think Struthiomimus was one of the fastest. It was 13 feet (4 m) long, looked like an ostrich, and may have reached speeds of 30 mph (50 km/h). Struthiomimus was an omnivore: it ate animals and plants. Its long claws could hook leaves and fruit from low trees. It also fed on insects and lizards.

PROJECT

MAKE A MEAT-EATER'S TOOTH

Model a big ball of self-hardening clay into the shape of a meat-eating dinosaur's tooth. Texture the surface and mark it so that it looks ancient and fossilized. It may take up to two days for the tooth to harden. When it is hard, paint your ferocious tooth.

❖ **Oviraptor** *had a tall crest on the top of its head. This birdlike creature fed on other dinosaurs' eggs, which it scooped up in its three-fingered hands and cracked open with its strong jaws. Oviraptors were about 6 feet (2 m) long.*

Plant-eating Dinosaurs

The dinosaur herbivores, or plant-eaters, fed on the vegetation they could reach.

Small herbivores, such as the cat-sized Scutellosaurus, for example, ate roots and plants on the ground. It had rows of bony studs along its back and tail to protect it from attack by larger meat-eaters. The long-necked sauropods, however, spent nearly all their time eating leaves from the treetops.

♦ **Long-necked plant-eaters** *such as Diplodocus may have reared up to reach the highest treetops. Diplodocus picked leaves with its front teeth, but had no back teeth for chewing.*

WHICH HAD THE LONGEST NECK?

Mamenchisaurus, a huge plant-eater found in China, had the longest neck of any animal ever known. Its neck was 50 feet (15 m) long—longer than eight tall men lying head to toe!

◆ **Iguanodon** *was a large, heavy dinosaur. A peaceful plant-eater, it could stand and walk either on its back legs or on all fours. It had spiked thumbs, which it may have used to defend itself if it was attacked by a hungry meat-eater.*

◆ **Diplodocus** *was about 90 feet (27 m) long and weighed 13 tons. The first skeleton was found in Wyoming, in 1899. Its whiplash tail was longer than its neck, and had more than 80 bones. But even bigger was Ultrasaurus, at about 100 feet (30 m) long.*

PROJECT

DIG UP A DIPLODOCUS

Cut up straws for bones and make them into a complete skeleton on a cardboard base. Brush each straw with glue and fix it firmly into position. Leave the straws to dry, and then brush more glue between the bones and around the whole skeleton. Sprinkle all over with sand. After a few minutes, tip the surplus sand onto newspaper. Then you'll have your very own fossilized Diplodocus!

Warm- or Cold-Blooded Creatures?

Today's reptiles are cold-blooded. This means their body warmth changes with the temperature of their surroundings. They have to wait for the Sun to warm them up before they can move about. Scientists used to think dinosaurs were cold-blooded. But were they?

Some scientists say that the long-necked dinosaurs must have been warm-blooded, because they would need high blood pressure to push the blood up to their brains.

In recent years it has been suggested that in fact *all* dinosaurs were warm-blooded. If they were, it meant their bodies stayed warm, because they got heat and energy from the food they ate. It certainly seems that they did not cool down and become slower like a modern-day reptile.

⬖ **Plated dinosaurs** *such as Tuojiangosaurus may have used the bony plates on their backs to soak up the Sun's heat and warm themselves up. So they may have been cold-blooded.*

◀ **If plant-eaters** *like this Lufengosaurus were warm-blooded, they must have eaten vast amounts of food. Warm-blooded animals need to eat more food so they can keep warm.*

▶ **The cold-blooded Komodo dragon** *is the biggest lizard alive today. It grows up to 10 feet (3 m) long. Being cold-blooded, it needs to eat its own weight in food only every two months. A warm-blooded lion needs to eat its own weight in food every week.*

PROJECT — CATCH-A-DINOSAUR GAME

Cut dinosaur shapes out of cardboard. Make slits to fit the dinosaurs onto plastic pots. Put sand in the pots to make them stable. Then throw a ball into a pot to catch a dinosaur!

Where Dinosaurs Lived

Tyrannosaurus

Dinosaur remains have been found all over the world. In fact, similar dinosaurs have been found on different continents, yet we know that they were land animals and could not have swum across vast oceans.

During the Age of Dinosaurs the continents were slowly drifting apart from the original supercontinent. So the dinosaurs could have crossed from one continent to another by land early on.

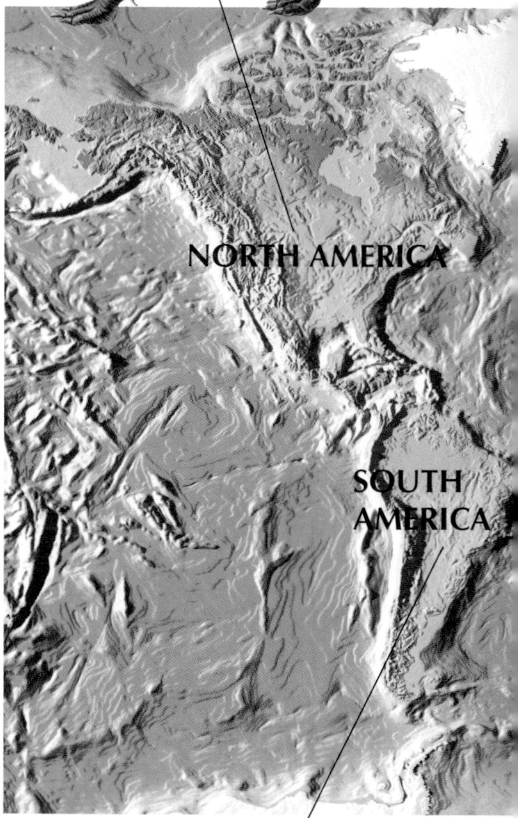

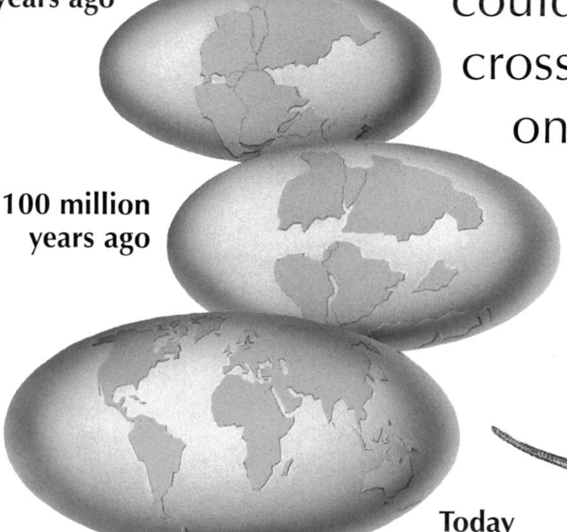

200 million years ago

100 million years ago

Today

NORTH AMERICA

SOUTH AMERICA

◆ **The continents** were once joined together as a supercontinent. But during the 165 million years that dinosaurs lived, the continents were drifting apart, so dinosaurs spread around the globe.

Staurikosaurus

Part of Dinosaur National Monument, in the western USA. It was in this region that Edward Cope and Othniel Marsh made great dinosaur finds about 100 years ago.

Iguanodon

Tuojiangosaurus

EUROPE   ASIA

AFRICA

AUSTRALIA

Minmi

This map of the world shows where major finds have been made. Dinosaur remains are still being found all the time.

Barosaurus

Famous dinosaur collectors:
1 Dr Robert Plot; 2 Mary Mantell;
3 Dr. Gideon Mantell; 4 Sir Richard Owen;
5 Edward Cope; 6 Othniel Marsh.

187

Moving Herds

We have learned a lot about how dinosaurs lived from the discovery of fossil footprints. These show how dinosaurs moved, and whether they traveled alone, in small groups, or in larger herds.

Apatosaurus was one of the large plant-eaters. From footprints found in

◊ **These dinosaur tracks** *were found in Queensland, Australia. At the time of the dinosaurs, Australia was moving away from Antarctica.*

Texas—all made at the same time, 150 million years ago—we know that these dinosaurs roamed across the North American plains in herds, possibly at a similar speed to modern elephants. Herds of up to 100 plant-eaters may have traveled long distances in search of food. Some tracks have shown that smaller, younger dinosaurs walked in the middle of the herd, where they were safe from attack.

MAKING FOOTPRINTS

PROJECT Pour paint into a baking tin or something similar. Put this at one end of some spread-out newspapers, and put a bucket of water and a towel at the other end. Then step into the paint, walk across the paper, and wash your feet in the water. Ask a friend to do the same, and compare the prints.

◊ **Hypsilophodon** *were small, fast plant-eaters that lived in herds. The first known Hypsilophodon was found in 1849. At that time it was wrongly thought to be a common Iguanodon.*

The Tarbosaurus, *found in China, is so similar to the Tyrannosaurus, found in North America, that they must have been very close relatives.*

Tyrannosaurus

Tarbosaurus

A herd of Apatosaurus *on the move. For many years, most scientists thought that these dinosaurs lived in water, using their long necks like snorkels. The footprint finds proved this to be quite wrong.*

Dinosaurs *such as Parasaurolophus and Saurolophus had head balloons and crests. They may have used these to increase the noises they made to warn other herd members of any dangers.*

Eggs and Nests

Female dinosaurs may have looked different from males, especially in their coloring. Two slightly different kinds of the same dinosaur have been found, and some scientists think these may have been males and females.

Female dinosaurs laid eggs, just like modern reptiles. The eggs had leathery shells to protect the babies. They were often laid in mud nests or hollows, which the mothers covered with plants or sand. We know this from the fossilized eggs that have been found. The first fossilized eggs were discovered in the Gobi Desert in Mongolia in 1923.

We also know that some groups of dinosaurs built their nests close together, in colonies. Scientists think some dinosaurs may have returned to the same nesting place year after year.

◐ **A mother Protoceratops** *watches as her tiny babies hatch from their eggs. Mothers may have stayed to help feed and protect their young until they were able to fend for themselves.*

HOW BIG?

The biggest dinosaur eggs found so far were 12 inches (30 cm) long—only six times bigger than a chicken's egg.

◑ **Today's crocodiles** *behave in a way that is probably very similar to dinosaurs. They make nests and cover them over with plants and mud, which help keep the eggs warm. When the babies hatch, mother carries them gently in her jaws to a nearby pool.*

◑ **Maiasaura**, *which means "good mother lizard," was so-named when a group of its nests were found with babies and fossilized eggs still inside. The mothers had scooped out mud nests about 6 feet (2 m) across and laid up to 20 eggs, each about 8 inches (20 cm) long, inside the hollows. They had then covered the eggs.*

Helmets, Spines, and Armor

Big, slow-moving animals needed to protect themselves against fast, fierce meat-eaters. Many plant-eating dinosaurs had some form of armor-plating to offer protection.

Some dinosaurs had plates and spines running down their backs and tails. Others had spikes that grew in their skin. Some even had bony clubs at the ends of their tails, which they used as weapons against attackers. Dinosaur skulls were filled mainly with muscle and bone. One group used their skulls to head-butt each other during fights.

◀ Styracosaurus *had long spikes sticking out of a bony frill. It also had a large nose horn, like a modern rhinoceros. It lived about 75 million years ago. Fossils have been found in the USA and Canada.*

PROJECT

◖ **Triceratops** *means "three-horned face."
Although the horns were for self-defence,
scientists think that these dinosaurs
may also have fought one another.
Triceratops' teeth were hard on
one side. The other, softer side
wore down faster, leaving a
sharp cutting edge.*

◖ **Euoplocephalus** *had slabs of bony armor,
spikes on its back, and a clubbed tail. It
used its powerful muscles to swing its
tail at any enemies.*

◖ **The largest
bone-headed dinosaur,**
*Pachycephalosaurus, had a thick, dome-shaped skull.
This head-butting creature was 15 feet (4.6 m) long.*

MAKE A SPIKY DINOSAUR

To make your own dinosaur, cut the sides off some large
cardboard boxes and tape them together. Draw a long dinosaur
body shape on the cardboard and cut it out. On another piece of
card, draw some plates for the dinosaur's back and some spikes
for its tail, cut these out, and fasten them with tape to the
body. Next, cut up some egg cartons to use for bony
bumps. Paint them green and tape them to the body.
Finally, crush up lots of pieces of tissue paper and glue
them all over your dinosaur's body. You could use a bottle-top for
a beady, prehistoric eye!

Other Giant Reptiles

During the long Age of Dinosaurs, other giant reptiles lived in the world's oceans.

Like their dinosaur cousins, sea reptiles breathed air. This meant that they had to come to the surface regularly to fill their lungs. Their air-filled lungs made it difficult for plesiosaurs to dive deep under water to catch their prey. To weigh themselves down, they swallowed stones.

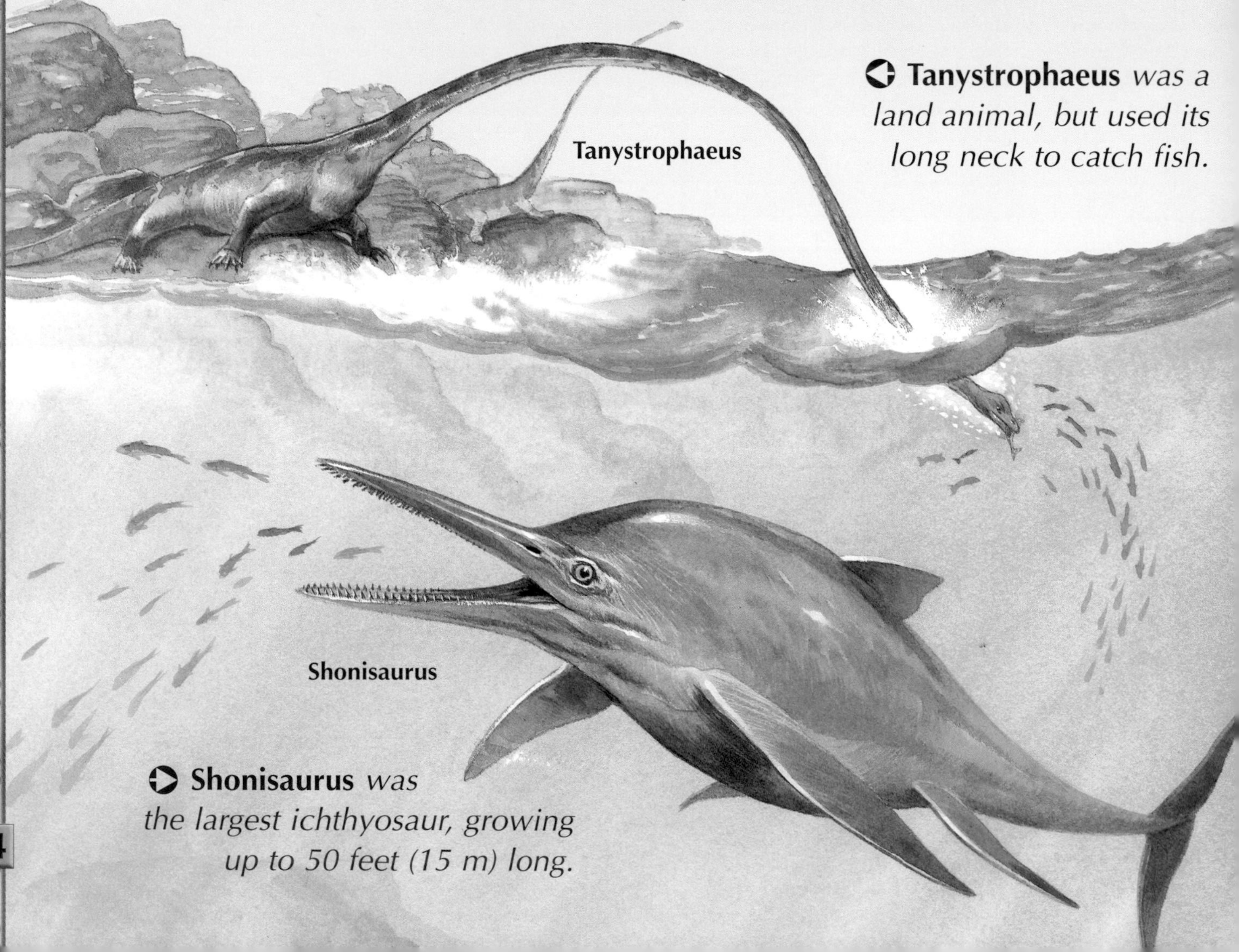

Tanystrophaeus

◐ **Tanystrophaeus** *was a land animal, but used its long neck to catch fish.*

Shonisaurus

◑ **Shonisaurus** *was the largest ichthyosaur, growing up to 50 feet (15 m) long.*

Crocodiles do the same today. Sea reptiles may have laid eggs in sandy nests on the shore. Ichthyosaurs were also reptiles, but gave birth to live young at sea.

◑ **Elasmosaurus** *was about 43 feet (13 m) in length, making it the longest of the long-necked plesiosaurs. Kronosaurus was a huge pliosaur with massive, sharp teeth. And Archelon was a giant turtle, almost 13 feet (4 m) long. All three sea reptiles lived toward the end of the Age of Dinosaurs.*

◑ **Deinosuchus** *was the largest crocodile that ever lived. It was up to 40 feet (12 m) long and had massive jaws. It swam in rivers and swamps, and may have fed on land animals coming there to drink.*

Elasmosaurus

Kronosaurus

Archelon

Into the Air

Reptiles took to the air over 200 million years ago. While dinosaurs ruled the land, pterosaurs were masters of the skies long before the first birds took off.

Pterosaurs flew on wings of skin, which stretched out from their bodies along their arms to their long fingers. They launched themselves from high cliffs and flapped their wings as they rode the air currents. They had light, delicate bones, which made it possible to stay in the air. Scientists believe they may have had fur to keep them warm, and may have been warm-blooded. They had larger brains than many dinosaurs.

Icarosaurus

Coelurosauravus

◆ **Pteranodons** *flew over the seas and used their long, toothless beaks to catch fish. They had a wing span of more than 16 feet (5 m). The long bony crest at the back of their heads may have been used as a rudder, guiding and balancing them as they flew. Fossils of Pteranodon have been dated at about 80 million years old.*

◆ **Icarosaurus and Coelurosauravus** *were early lizardlike animals with wings. Icarosaurus lived over 200 million years ago. It climbed trees, with its wings folded against its body. Then it launched itself off, and its thin wings helped it glide through the air.*

DARTING THROUGH THE AIR

PROJECT

You can easily make a pterosaur flier from a sheet of paper. Take a piece of paper and fold toward the center. When you've finished folding, use a drop of glue to hold the flier's body together. Don't forget to draw on some sharp pterosaur eyes and color in the wings, following some of the colors on this page. Now launch your flying pterosaur on a journey into the sky!

The largest pterosaur *yet discovered, called Quetzalcoatlus, had a wingspan of about 40 feet (12 m). It may have weighed as much as a big man.*

Rhamphorhynchus *lived about 145 million years ago. It had a narrow head and pointed teeth. Its long tail probably helped it to balance and change direction in mid-air.*

Dimorphodon *had a large, heavy head and was probably a clumsy flier. It may have glided for short distances between trees and rocks.*

197

The First Birds

One of the earliest birdlike reptiles is Archaeopteryx, which lived about 150 million years ago. It was probably a close relative of the dinosaurs, but it had feathers, like a bird, and it could fly a little.

The name Archaeopteryx means "ancient wing." It was about the size of a chicken, and had a long tail and long legs. It probably climbed more than it flew.

About 90 million years ago, while dinosaurs still roamed the land, water birds were starting to catch fish in the sea. Some of these flying creatures may still have been more at home in the water than they were on land or in the air.

⚫ The first fossils of **Archaeopteryx** *were found in southern Germany in 1861. They showed the feather impressions so clearly that scientists thought the find was a hoax.*

beak with teeth

clawed fingers

⚫ **Archaeopteryx** *probably pulled itself up tall trees by its claws and launched itself into flight from the top. It may have eaten insects and other small animals.*

bony tail

WHAT COLOR?
We don't know what color the first birds were. Fossil feathers show us shape and size, but not color. Males and females may have been different colors.

▶ **Diatryma** *was a fast-running flightless bird with a large, parrotlike beak and big claws. It was as big as a tall human and lived about 50 million years ago. Diatryma may have chased the first small horses.*

▶ **Hesperornis** *was a good underwater swimmer, but probably could not fly.*

▶ **Ichthyornis** *was like a modern gull and could fly to catch fish.*

Hesperornis

Ichthyornis

199

Dinosaurs Die Out

Dinosaurs became extinct, or died out, about 65 million years ago. The great reptiles of the sea and air disappeared at the same time. We are not sure why this happened.

It could be that the Earth became covered in volcanic dust and smoke, which blocked out sunlight for many months. Plants and many animals would not have been able to survive such a catastrophe.

⬦ **The plant-eater Saltasaurus** was one of the last known dinosaurs. Once the plant-eaters had died out, the meat-eaters ran out of food!

⬦ **It could be that many vast volcanoes** erupted over a few years or even longer. This may have made the Earth too hot, poisoned the air, and blotted out the Sun.

This Meteor Crater in Arizona was made about 50,000 years ago, when a meteorite hit Earth. Some scientists think a much bigger asteroid may have struck Earth 65 million years ago, causing the dust that blocked out the Sun and killed the dinosaurs.

If we had not found fossilized bones, we may never have known that dinosaurs ever existed.

DID ALL THE EGGS DISAPPEAR?

Another theory is that small mammals raided dinosaur nests and ate so many eggs all at once that there were no more dinosaur babies. This seems an unlikely story.

201

Mammals Take Over

The first mammals appeared about 200 million years ago. During the time that dinosaurs ruled the land, mammals remained very small.

⬥ **Morganucodon** (on the left) and Deltatheridium (on the right) were small, very early mammals. It's easy to see why we compare them to modern shrews.

Most early mammals probably stayed in burrows during the day, coming out to feed at night when larger animals were asleep. But when the dinosaurs died out, the warm-blooded mammals took over the land. They grew bigger and more powerful, and some became meat-eaters.

An enormous mammal was Uintatherium. It was rather like today's rhinoceros. It measured 13 feet (4 m) long and had six big, hornlike bony knobs on its head.

⬣ **This scene shows** what the world may have looked like about 40 million years ago. Mammals like today's elephants, bears, horses, and bats were starting to rule the land and compete with each other.

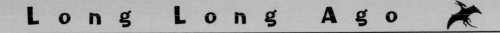

DRAW A MIXED-UP MAMMAL

PROJECT

How many different mammals can you spot in this one drawing? You could draw your own mixed-up mammal. Find pictures of your favorite animals earlier in the encyclopedia and draw different parts of them, mixing up the heads, bodies, legs, and arms. Any combination is possible, and you could do the same with dinosaurs and other reptiles.

◗ **The common tree shrew** *is probably quite similar to the very early mammals that existed in the time of the dinosaurs. Shrews are found in most parts of the world.*

◗ **Pantolambda** *was an early hoofed plant-eater, about the size of a modern sheep. It may have spent some of its time wallowing in the mud, just like a modern-day hippopotamus.*

Early Man

Humanlike creatures that we call "southern apes" lived in Africa about four million years ago. We know that about two million years later, a kind of human that we call "handy man" was making and using stone tools.

Hundreds of thousands of years after that, "upright man" found out how to use fire. Next came Neanderthal man. He evolved about 250,000 years ago, and died out about 30,000 years ago. By this time, another human being was around. This was "modern man," or Homo sapiens, which means "wise man." He developed farming, kept animals, and made cave paintings.

Most prehistoric people hunted large animals such as mammoths, and gathered fruits, berries, and nuts to eat.

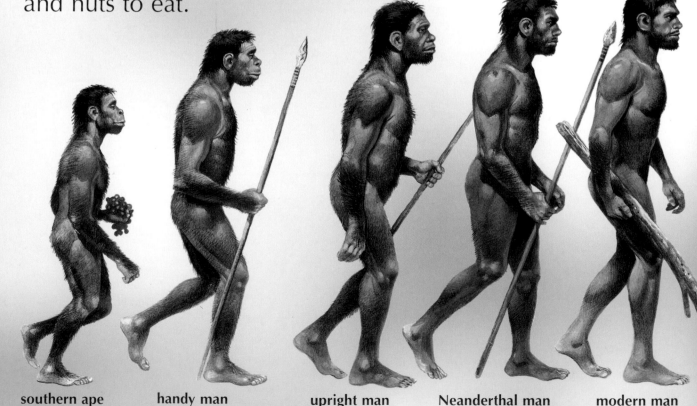

southern ape   handy man   upright man   Neanderthal man   modern man

STONE PAINTINGS

You can turn a collection of smooth pebbles or stones into a friendly snake. Give your stones a good wash and then let them dry thoroughly before you start painting. Use the biggest stone for the head, and then go down in size all the way to the tip of the tail. Paint the body of your snake with green poster paint, and let this dry before adding yellow markings, a pair of eyes, and a forked tongue. When the stones are dry, arrange them into a slithering snake shape.

PROJECT

◑ **Prehistoric paintings** *in caves at Lascaux, France, were found by four teenage boys in 1940. The paintings of animals were made about 17,000 years ago.*

◑ **The early, humanlike "southern ape"** or *Australopithecus was small. Next came "handy man" (Homo habilis), who could make stone tools, then "upright man," who used fire. We modern humans are from the group called "wise man" (Homo sapiens).*

◑ **We think that Homo erectus,** or *"upright man," was the first to use fire. This was useful for cooking food, keeping warm, and scaring away animals from shelters such as caves. Hot stones may have been arranged in the fire to make simple ovens.*

205

Discovering Dinosaurs

The dinosaurs died out many millions of years before the first humans walked on Earth. When people first found dinosaur bones and fossils, they didn't know what they were.

Less than 200 years ago, scientists realized that they belonged to extinct reptiles, and in 1841 British scientist Sir Richard Owen gave them the name "dinosaurs." Since then scientists called paleontologists have studied many thousands of fossils carefully.

⬥ **Some prehistoric insects** *were trapped in amber, made from a sticky substance that oozes from the trunks of some trees and hardens.*

⬥ **When dinosaurs died,** *their bones were covered in mud. This hardened into rock as more layers of mud built up on top. Over millions of years, the rock wore away again to reveal fossilized bones.*

◀ **These bones of the plant-eater Hypacrosaurus** *show the shape of the animal very clearly. Fossil bones are usually found near each other, but often have to be put together like a jigsaw puzzle.*

They have put together the picture of prehistoric life that we have today. Dinosaur names are usually given in Latin. Many of the names describe a particular animal's appearance. So Euoplocephalus means "well-armored head."

⬧ **Paleontologists** *keep detailed notes on where bones are found. They take photographs and make drawings and diagrams before the bones are taken away from the original site. Other scientists can learn a lot from these original notes.*

⬧ **First dirt has to be brushed** *from bones. Then each bone is labeled and given a number. This helps when putting the pieces together later.*

⬧ **Bones are carefully wrapped** *in wet plaster before they are moved from the original site. When the plaster has hardened, the bones can safely be taken to a laboratory. The plaster jacket that protected them can then be taken off, so that scientists can test and study the bones.*

Quiz

1. Did the first fishes suck in food or bite it? (page 170)

2. How many different kinds of seaweed are there today? (page 171)

3. Which famous scientist traveled to South America in 1832? (page 172)

4. The first horse was only as big as which modern animal? (page 172)

5. Where do amphibians lay their eggs? (page 174)

6. What does "amphibian" mean? (page 174)

7. Were early reptiles able to live on land all the time? (page 176)

8. What did sail-backed reptiles use their sail for? (page 177)

9. What does the word "dinosaur" mean? (page 178)

10. When did the first dinosaurs appear on Earth? (page 178)

11. What was the name of an egg-snatching dinosaur? (page 181)

12. What bird did Struthiomimus look like? (page 181)

13. What is a herbivore? (page 182)

14. How long was Diplodocus? (page 183)

15. What warms reptiles up each morning? (page 184)

16. Which is the biggest lizard alive today? (page 185)

17. What do we call the huge mass of land that the continents split from? (page 186)

18. Where did the famous dinosaur collectors Cope and Marsh make great finds? (page 187)

19. Why did young dinosaurs walk in the middle of the herd? (page 188)

20. In which American state were Apatosaurus footprints found? (page 188)

21. Where were the first dinosaur eggs found? (page 190)

22. What does the name "Maiasaura" mean? (page 191)

23. What did Pachycephalosaurus do with its head? (page 193)

24. Which dinosaur had a "three-horned face"? (page 193)

25. How long was the largest crocodile that ever lived? (page 195)

26. What did plesiosaurs swallow to weigh themselves down? (page 195)

27. What may pteranodons have used their head crests for? (page 196)

28. How big was the wingspan of the largest pterosaur? (page 197)

29. When did the first bird live? (page 198)

30. What did Archaeopteryx use its claws for? (page 198)

31. When did dinosaurs die out? (page 200)

32. Where is Meteor Crater? (page 201)

33. Which modern animal is similar to the very early mammals? (page 202)

34. What did Uintatherium have on its head? (page 202)

35. Who do we think was first to use fire? (page 204)

36. Which came first, "upright man" or "handy man"? (page 204)

37. Were there humans alive at the same time as dinosaurs? (page 206)

38. What do scientists wrap dinosaur bones in? (page 207)

People and Places

The people of the world live on six different continents. Each of these continents has its own special landscapes and famous places, all of which have developed in their own unique way throughout history. Humans live in rainforests and deserts, near oceans and rivers, in small villages as well as gigantic, crowded cities.

All the world's people belong to the same human race, despite being split up into hundreds of nations and other groups. Many of these groups have their own language, religion, festivals, and customs, all based on their own special history. We can all learn by studying how other people live, all over the world.

North America

The continent of North America stretches all the way from the frozen Arctic Ocean in the north to the warm waters of the Caribbean Sea in the south. It includes two of the biggest countries in the world, Canada and the United States of America.

◑ **The Grand Canyon,** *in Arizona, is the largest gorge in the world. It is about 210 miles (350 km) long and 1.2 miles (2 km) deep.*

The land varies from the freezing icecaps of Greenland to the huge, cold forests of Canada, from the American prairies and the deserts of northern Mexico, to the tropical rainforests of Central America. The Rocky Mountains run almost all the way down the western side of the continent, while New York City—the largest city in the United States—is on the eastern side.

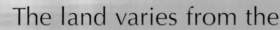

◐ **In New York City,** *the crowded island of Manhattan is one of the city's five boroughs. It is surrounded by three rivers. Bridges and tunnels link it with the rest of the city.*

○ **Greenland** (far right) is the largest island in the world. Most of its land lies within the Arctic Circle.

Greenland (DENMARK)

ALASKA (USA)

Yukon

Mackenzie

CANADA

Hudson Bay

Newfoundland

○ Alaska is the largest of the 50 states that make up the USA, but it has the smallest population. Like Canada and Greenland, it has lots of ice and snow.

Edmonton

Vancouver

Missouri

Snake

Missouri

Montreal

Ottawa

Great Lakes

Toronto

Boston

Detroit

New York City

Chicago

Philadelphia

Washington D.C.

San Francisco

Ohio

ATLANTIC OCEAN

UNITED STATES OF AMERICA

Los Angeles

Mississippi

PACIFIC OCEAN

Colorado

Dallas

Houston

New Orleans

Rio Grande

Miami

BAHAMAS

Puerto Rico (U.S.)

Monterrey

GULF OF MEXICO

Havana

CUBA

DOMINICAN REPUBLIC

MEXICO

HAITI

Guadalajara

JAMAICA

CARIBBEAN SEA

Mexico City

BELIZE

GUATEMALA

HONDURAS

EL SALVADOR

NICARAGUA

COSTA RICA

PANAMA

SOUTH AMERICA

○ **This Mexican pyramid** was built more than 1,000 years ago by a Native American people named the Maya. The pyramid was a temple to their god Kukulcan.

211

North American People

Many thousands of years ago, hunters from northeast Asia crossed a land bridge to the region that is now named Alaska. The descendants of these people gradually spread southward, across the whole of the continent.

◐ **The Inuit** *live in northern Canada and Greenland. In their own language, Inuit just means "people."*

About 1,000 years ago, Viking explorers sailed to North America from Europe. But it was only about 500 years ago that Europeans first made permanent settlements there.

The USA forms a single nation with its own way of life, but it is made up of people who came to live there from all over the world.

On the fourth Thursday in November, Americans celebrate Thanksgiving. Early settlers "gave thanks" for surviving in the New World.

◑ **Native people** *who lived along the northwest Pacific coast of Canada and the USA carved beautiful totem poles outside their homes.*

WHEN DID A RAILROAD FIRST CROSS AMERICA?

On May 10, 1869, a Union Pacific construction locomotive met one from the Central Pacific line, at a place called Promontory, in Utah. This completed a track that ran right across the United States.

❯ Football *grew from the British sport of rugby more than 100 years ago. The best college stars go on to play in the NFL.*

FEATHER HEADDRESS

PROJECT Cut a strip of corrugated paper and fit it around your head. Stick the ends together with parcel tape. Tear colored tissue into small pieces, crumple them up and glue them to the outside. Cut feather shapes from tissue and glue each one onto a plastic straw. Then slot the ends into the corrugated holes.

◗ Mexicans *celebrate many public holidays with "fiestas." Many people dress up and dance in the streets.*

◆ Riding a bucking bronco *is one of the skills that cowboys display at rodeos. Years ago, cowboys drove huge herds of cattle to railroad towns. It was a hard life and not nearly as exciting as it looks in cowboy films!*

South America

The continent of South America is divided into 13 countries. By far the largest of these countries is Brazil, which covers nearly half the continent's total area.

The Andes Mountains stretch down almost the whole of South America. They form the longest mountain range in the world. The great Amazon River begins high in the Andes of Peru. It flows across the plains of Brazil, through the world's biggest rainforest, to the Atlantic Ocean.

◖ **A huge statue of Christ** *looks down on the city and crowded beaches of Rio de Janeiro, in Brazil. The statue stands 132 feet (40 m) high.*

◖ **In the Amazon rainforest,** *parrots and toucans feed in the treetops, and monkeys swing through the branches. Many of the rainforest animals are losing their homes as trees are cut down for timber.*

214

◐ **The Andes mountain range** is 4,470 miles (7,200 km) long. The highest point, Aconcagua, is in Argentina.

◑ **The ruins** of the Inca town of Machu Picchu are perched high above a river valley in the Andes of Peru. A royal palace and a temple are among the ruins.

◑ **The southern tip** of the continent is Cape Horn. It was named in 1616 by a Dutch explorer, after his home town of Hoorn in Holland, and is usually very stormy.

◑ **Llamas** are members of the camel family. They have been bred in Peru for thousands of years, for their wool and to carry things.

Map labels:

Caribbean Sea
Caracas
VENEZUELA
Bogotá
COLOMBIA
Orinoco
GUYANA
SURINAM
FRENCH GUYANA
Negro
Quito
ECUADOR
Marañón
Amazon
Madeira
Xingu
Tocantins
PERU
B R A Z I L
Lima
Brasília
BOLIVIA
PACIFIC OCEAN
Paraguay
PARAGUAY
São Paulo
Rio de Janeiro
CHILE
Asunción
ARGENTINA
URUGUAY
Buenos Aires
Montevideo
Santiago
Colorado
ATLANTIC OCEAN
Falkland Islands (U.K.)
Tierra del Fuego
Cape Horn

South American People

The first Europeans arrived in South America in the 16th century. They then conquered and destroyed the powerful Native American cultures they found there. The cultures included that of the mighty Inca empire.

BIG OR LITTLE RAIN?

So much rain falls in the rainforest around the Amazon that Brazilians divide the seasons into times of "big rains" and "little rains." All this rain means that more than one fifth of all the water in the world's rivers flows down the River Amazon.

Today, most South Americans are descended from Europeans and Indians, or Native Americans, and many are a mixture of the two. Spanish is the continent's main language, but in the largest country,

◆ **The mountain people** of the Andes spin the wool they get from their llamas and sheep into yarn, dye it, and weave it into brightly colored blankets, shawls, and skirts.

◐ **Brazil** *is famous for its friendly, crowded carnivals. They draw thousands of tourists every year. Many of the locals dress up in colorful costumes.*

◑ **Gauchos** *are Argentinian cowboys, famous for their horsemanship. They herd cattle on grassy plains called pampas.*

Brazil, people speak Portuguese. Hundreds of Indian languages are also spoken by the different Native American peoples.

Soccer is the most popular sport in South America. Brazil has won the World Cup five times, and Uruguay and Argentina twice each.

MAKE A SHAKER

PROJECT Use an empty dishwashing liquid bottle or something similar. Put in some dried beans and push a stick into the neck of the bottle. Tape the stick so that it fits tightly. Paint the shaker with powder or poster paints mixed with a teaspoon of dishwashing liquid. Stick on some tissue-paper decorations with glue. Then shake to a South American beat.

◑ **The Aymara people** *traditionally live by farming and fishing from reed boats on Lake Titicaca. The lake lies high in the Andes, between Peru and Bolivia.*

217

Europe

The northern parts of Europe are mainly cold regions. They include Scandinavia, which is made up of Norway, Sweden, Finland, Denmark, and Iceland. The central parts of the continent are mild, while the southern regions surrounding the Mediterranean Sea are mainly warm and dry. Europe has a rugged coastline, dotted with many small islands.

❍ **In the Middle Ages in Europe,** *kings and lords lived in castles, which were designed to be difficult for an enemy to attack. Many different types of castle can still be seen in Europe today.*

⬥ **There are many active geysers,** *or hot springs, in Iceland. They regularly throw boiling hot water and steam high up into the air. Icelanders use hot water from beneath the Earth's surface to run power plants and heat their homes.*

A popular tourist beach on one of Greece's many small islands. In the summer it is warm and sunny all around the coast of the Mediterranean Sea.

The road across Tower Bridge, in London, can be made to swing up to allow tall ships to pass through. Many of Europe's rivers are important waterways, carrying river traffic to and from distant seaports.

The western half of Russia (shown on this map) is in Europe. The rest of Russia is in Asia.

Reykjavik • ICELAND

NORWEGIAN SEA

SWEDEN
FINLAND
NORWAY
Oslo •
Stockholm •
Helsinki •
St. Petersburg •
R U S S I A
Archangel •

ATLANTIC OCEAN

NORTH SEA

DENMARK
Copenhagen •
ESTONIA
LATVIA
LITHUANIA
BALTIC SEA

Moscow •
Nizhniy Novgorod •

REP. OF IRELAND
Dublin •
UNITED KINGDOM
NETHERLANDS
London •
BELGIUM
Paris •
Seine
LUXEMBOURG
Loire
FRANCE
Lyon •
Bay of Biscay
SWITZERLAND
Rhône
Milan •
Po
GERMANY
Berlin •
CZECH REPUBLIC
Danube
Vienna •
AUSTRIA
SLOVENIA
SLOVAKIA
Budapest •
HUNGARY
CROATIA
BOSNIA HERZEGOVINA
POLAND
Warsaw •
BELARUS
Minsk •
UKRAINE
Kiev •
Dnieper
MOLDOVA
ROMANIA
Bucharest •
Don
KAZAKHSTAN
Volga

PORTUGAL
sbon •
Duero
Tagus
Madrid •
SPAIN
Seville •
Gibraltar •
ANDORRA
Barcelona •
Corsica
Sardinia
ITALY
Rome •
Naples •
SERBIA & MONTENEGRO
BULGARIA
Sofia •
MACEDONIA
ALBANIA
GREECE
Athens •
Istanbul •
BLACK SEA
Ankara •
ASIA
T U R K E Y

Balearic Islands (Spain)
Sicily
M E D I T E R R A N E A N   S E A

NORTH AFRICA

European People

Europe is full of many small countries and different peoples. Most have their own language and culture.

The north is home to Finns and Lapps, and to those who speak Germanic languages, such as the English, Dutch, and Germans. In the south, people speak French, Spanish, and Italian, which all came from Latin, the language of the ancient Romans. Within Rome (the capital of Italy), is Vatican City, the smallest country in the world.

◗ **Flamenco** *is a Spanish way of dancing and singing to guitar music. Dancers snap their fingers, clap their hands, and shout in time to the music.*

FAN YOURSELF

PROJECT

To make a Spanish fan, first paint or draw a bright pattern on a long sheet of paper. You could decorate it with glitter glue to add sparkle. When it is dry, fold the paper, making sure all the folds are the same size. Staple the folds at one end and attach a popsicle stick as a handle for your fancy fan.

◒ **A gondolier,** *or oarsman, steers his gondola along one of the many canals of Venice, in Italy. The water almost completely surrounds this beautiful city.*

◒ **This square is in Prague,** *the capital and largest city of the Czech Republic. The city's historic buildings attract many visitors all year round.*

◒ **Marching military bands** *are a traditional feature of British ceremonies. These soldiers are wearing fur helmets called "bearskins."*

◒ **The grape harvest** *is very important to winemakers in France, Italy, Spain, and other southern European countries. In the past, people stamped on the grapes to press out the juice, but today this is usually done by machine.*

Asia

Asia is by far the largest continent in the world, bigger than the whole of North and South America put together.

Asian landscapes range from the huge, cold forest that stretches across northern Russia to the warm, wet rainforests of the islands of Southeast Asia. The world's highest mountains are also to be found in Asia.

Russia is the largest country in the world. Crossing it all the way from Moscow to Vladivostok is the Trans-Siberian Railway. Trains go on from there to Beijing, China.

⬆ **The Great Wall of China** *was built to help keep out invaders from the north. It was begun about 200 BC.*

⬇ **The Himalayas,** *a mountain range to the north of India, contain many of the highest mountains in the world. The highest of all, Mount Everest, rises to 8,848 m. It lies between Nepal and Tibet, and was first climbed in 1953.*

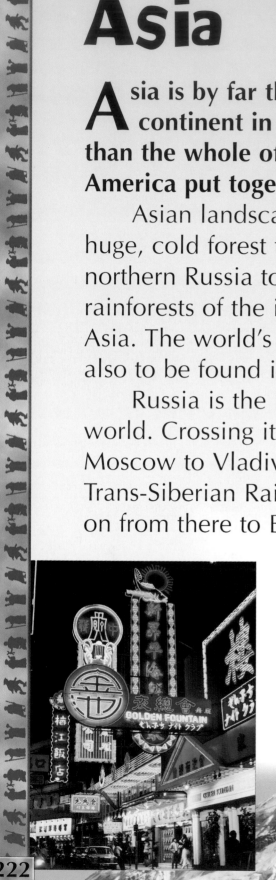

◐ **Hong Kong** *is an important port and city on the Chinese coast. This former British colony was returned to China in 1997.*

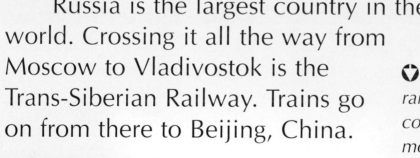

Japan (far right of map) has more than 3,900 islands. A legend tells how an ancient god dipped his spear into the ocean and formed the islands from the sunlit droplets of water.

Rice is an important food throughout Asia. It is grown in flooded paddy fields, like this one in Thailand. Sometimes fields are drained to help with harvesting.

223

Asian People

Over half the world's people live in Asia, which includes the country with more people than any other—China.

The world's first civilizations grew up in southwest Asia, in a fertile area between two great rivers, the Tigris and the Euphrates. There, farming started, and early cities developed.

In Indonesia, on the island of Borneo, many families of the Dayak people live together in wooden longhouses.

Brunei is a small country on the island of Borneo. The Sultan of Brunei is one of the richest people in the world. His palace has 1,788 rooms!

◑ **The Mongols** of northern China and Mongolia are expert horse riders. They follow their herds of goats and cattle across the grasslands, living in felt tents called yurts.

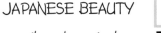

You can easily make a simple Japanese flower arrangement in a bowl. Cover the bottom of the clear bowl with soil, then add gravel, shells, and pebbles. Push a small twig through the gravel into the soil. Half-fill the bowl with water. Then decorate the surface with leaves and flowers, to make simple Japanese beauty.

⬥ **Very few people** *live in the dry, hot Arabian Desert, but some Bedouin nomads live on its margins, herding camel and cattle. Their tents provide welcome shade.*

⬥ **Sumo** *is the national wrestling sport of Japan. Sumo wrestlers are very big and strong, and try to throw down their opponent or force him out of the ring to win.*

⬥ **Fishermen in Sri Lanka** *sit on poles in the shallow sea to fish.*

⬥ **In China,** *bike riding is a popular way to get around the big cities quickly and easily. There are many large bicycle parks, with special attendants to look after them.*

Africa

Africa is the world's second largest continent. It is made up of 53 independent countries, some large and others small. The largest African country, Sudan, is more than 200 times bigger than the smallest, Gambia.

◊ **Mount Kilimanjaro** *rises to 19,340 feet (5,895 m) in Tanzania, and is Africa's highest mountain. The grasslands at the base are hot, but at the top it is cold enough for snow.*

The Sahara is the biggest desert in the world. It covers more than one fourth of Africa and stretches for more than 3,000 miles (5,000 km)—from the Atlantic Ocean to the Red Sea. Farther south, the land is much more fertile with rainforests and grasslands.

In 1869 the Suez Canal was opened, joining the Red Sea to the Mediterranean Sea. This meant that ships could sail from Europe to the Indian Ocean without having to go right around Africa. The canal is 105 miles (169 km) long. Thousands of ships pass through it every year.

◑ **The spectacular Victoria Falls** *plunge over a drop of 357 feet (108 m) on the Zambezi River, on the border between Zambia and Zimbabwe. The Falls' African name, Mosi oa Tunya, means "the smoke that thunders."*

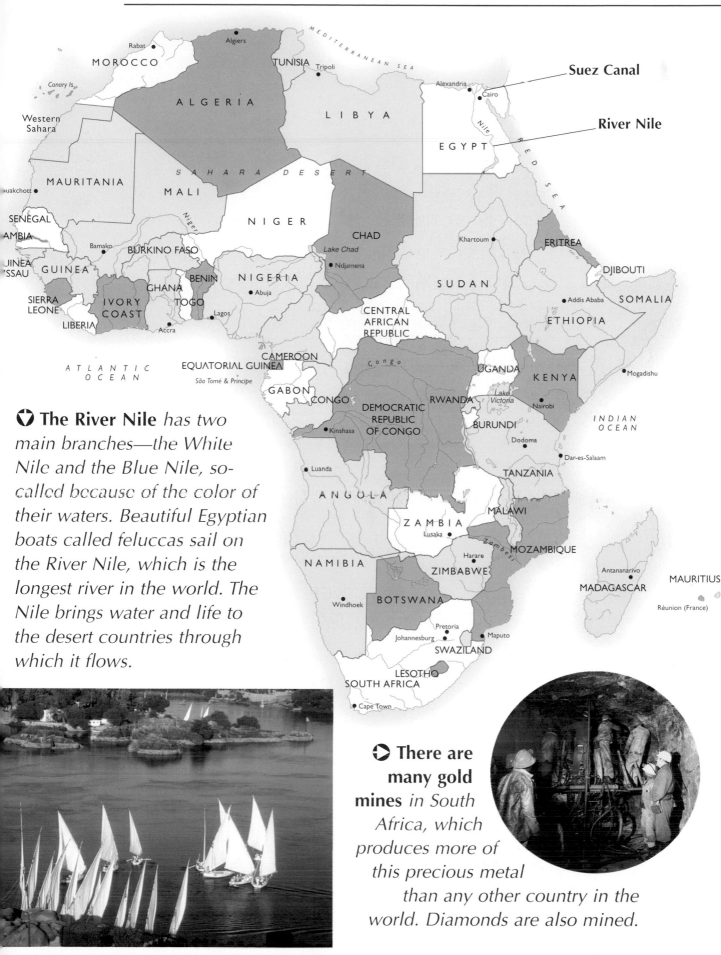

Suez Canal

River Nile

MOROCCO
Rabat
Algiers
TUNISIA
Tripoli
MEDITERRANEAN SEA
Alexandria
Cairo
ALGERIA
LIBYA
Canary Is.
Western Sahara
EGYPT
Nile
RED SEA
MAURITANIA
SAHARA DESERT
Khartoum
ERITREA
ouakchott
MALI
NIGER
CHAD
SENEGAL
Niger
Lake Chad
Ndjamena
SUDAN
DJIBOUTI
AMBIA
JINEA
'SSAU
Bamako
BURKINO FASO
SOMALIA
GUINEA
NIGERIA
Abuja
CENTRAL AFRICAN REPUBLIC
Addis Ababa
ETHIOPIA
SIERRA LEONE
IVORY COAST
GHANA
BENIN
TOGO
Lagos
LIBERIA
Accra
CAMEROON
ATLANTIC OCEAN
EQUATORIAL GUINEA
São Tomé & Principe
Congo
UGANDA
KENYA
Mogadishu
GABON
CONGO
DEMOCRATIC REPUBLIC OF CONGO
RWANDA
Lake Victoria
Nairobi
Kinshasa
BURUNDI
Dodoma
INDIAN OCEAN
Luanda
TANZANIA
Dar-es-Salaam
ANGOLA
MALAWI
ZAMBIA
Zambesi
MOZAMBIQUE
Lusaka
Harare
NAMIBIA
ZIMBABWE
Antananarivo
MAURITIUS
MADAGASCAR
BOTSWANA
Réunion (France)
Windhoek
Pretoria
Maputo
Johannesburg
SWAZILAND
LESOTHO
SOUTH AFRICA
Cape Town

◐ **The River Nile** *has two main branches—the White Nile and the Blue Nile, so-called because of the color of their waters. Beautiful Egyptian boats called feluccas sail on the River Nile, which is the longest river in the world. The Nile brings water and life to the desert countries through which it flows.*

◐ **There are many gold mines** *in South Africa, which produces more of this precious metal than any other country in the world. Diamonds are also mined.*

227

African People

Scientists believe that the earliest humans lived in Africa millions of years ago. During the 1800s and 1900s, many Africans were ruled by European colonizers.

Most Africans have always lived traditionally in villages and farmed the land. But the African population is growing very quickly, and many large cities have sprung up and continue to grow. Here there are modern offices and factories.

◀ **These Fulani women** *from West Africa carry bowls on their heads with ease. Traditionally the Fulani are cattle herders, but some have moved to the cities to find work.*

◀ **Johannesburg** *is the largest city in South Africa. About 4 million people live there. The city has many modern skyscrapers and shopping centers.*

▶ **The streets** *of many North African cities are very crowded, and there are bustling markets. Marrakech, a large city in Morocco, is well known for its leather goods and textiles. These, and the warm climate, make it popular with tourists.*

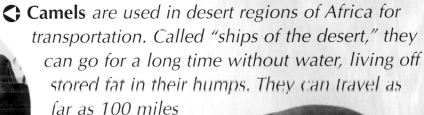

◀ **Camels** *are used in desert regions of Africa for transportation. Called "ships of the desert," they can go for a long time without water, living off stored fat in their humps. They can travel as far as 100 miles (160 km) a day.*

The Mbuti pygmies, who live in the Democratic Republic of the Congo (formerly Zaire), are thought to be the world's shortest people. The average man is only 58 inches (1.45 m) tall, and some Mbuti women measure just 49 inches (1.24 m).

▶ **Many Africans** *dress in a traditional way, according to the custom of their people.*

229

Australasia

The continent of Australasia is made up of Australia, New Zealand, Papua New Guinea, and thousands of small islands in the South Pacific Ocean. This region is sometimes called Oceania.

Australia is a warm, dry country. Much of its land is desert and dry bush country, called outback. New Zealand has a cooler climate. Both countries are home to many plants and animals seen nowhere else on Earth.

Papua New Guinea covers the eastern half of New Guinea. (The western half, called West Papua, belongs to Indonesia.)

The Pacific Islands are spread out over a vast area, but most of the islands themselves are tiny.

⬆ **The Great Barrier Reef** *lies off the eastern coast of Australia. It is made up of thousands of coral reefs. Corals look like plants, but are really made up of tiny, colorful animals related to jellyfish. The warm, shallow waters support many kinds of brightly colored fish.*

⬇ **Ayers Rock** *rises 1,143 feet (348 m) above the surrounding plain. This giant rock is sacred to the Aborigines, who call it Uluru, which means "Earth mother."*

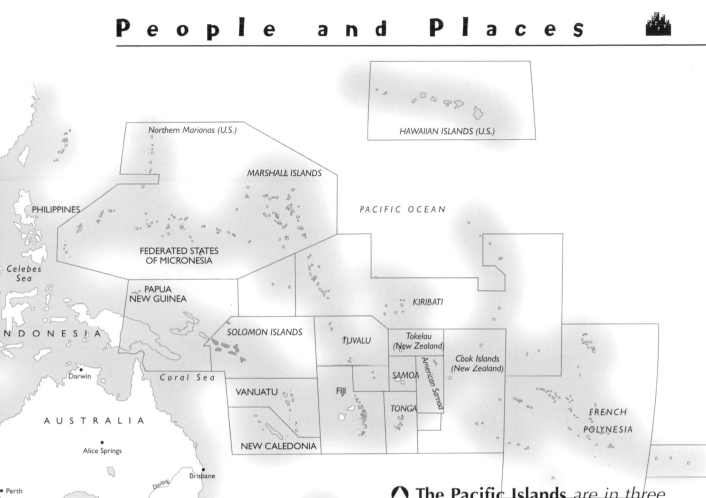

Northern Marianas (U.S.)

HAWAIIAN ISLANDS (U.S.)

MARSHALL ISLANDS

PACIFIC OCEAN

PHILIPPINES

FEDERATED STATES
OF MICRONESIA

Celebes
Sea

PAPUA
NEW GUINEA

KIRIBATI

INDONESIA

SOLOMON ISLANDS

TUVALU

Tokelau
(New Zealand)

Cook Islands
(New Zealand)

Darwin

Coral Sea

SAMOA

American Samoa

VANUATU

FIJI

FRENCH
POLYNESIA

AUSTRALIA

TONGA

Alice Springs

Darling

NEW CALEDONIA

Brisbane

• Perth

Sydney

Adelaide

Canberra

Aukland

Melbourne

Tasman Sea

Wellington

Tasmania

NEW ZEALAND

◆ **The Pacific Islands** *are in three main groups—Micronesia, which means "small islands," Melanesia ("black islands"), and Polynesia, meaning "many islands."*

◆ **The roof of the Sydney Opera House** *looks like giant sails. Sydney is the oldest and biggest city in Australia.*

WHICH LAKE HAS NO WATER?

Lake Eyre, Australia's largest lake, is normally a huge area of mud covered with a crust of salt. This is because the water dries up in the heat of the desert. When there is very heavy rainfall, the lake does fill with water, but this is rare.

Australasian People

Australia is the sixth biggest country in the world, but only 18 million people live there. Much of the land is hot, dry desert. Most people live along the coasts.

The first Australians were Aborigines, who came from Asia about 40,000 years ago. They probably crossed land that is now under water, and wandered the desert, hunting and gathering food. The first European settlers arrived in 1788 and founded the city of Sydney.

Maoris were the first New Zealanders. A Maori legend tells how they sailed there from Polynesia in just seven canoes.

◑ **Cricket** *is a very popular sport in Australia and New Zealand. Many celebrated players have come from these two countries.*

◐ **Australians** *love the outdoor life. Surfing is popular off many beaches, along with swimming and sailing.*

Wood carving *is a traditional craft of the Maoris of New Zealand. The carvings decorate Maori meeting houses. Today, much of the work is done to sell to tourists.*

WHAT DAY IS IT?

The international date line is an imaginary line that runs between the Pacific islands. On the western side of the line, it is exactly a day later than on the eastern side. So when it is midday Friday in Fiji, it is midday Thursday in Western Samoa.

Mudmen *of New Guinea wear masks made of dried mud for special ceremonies. They try to look really scary! More than 700 languages are spoken by the people of Papua New Guinea. Pidgin English and Motu are the most common.*

Australian Aborigines *tell stories in their rock paintings. Many have been found that are thousands of years old.*

Aborigines *play a long, thick wooden pipe called a didgeridoo. This makes a deep note, which the player can make louder by resting the end of the pipe over a hole in the ground. A boomerang, or throwing stick, is another traditional item.*

Ancient Egypt

Thousands of years ago, people hunted around the River Nile. Then they settled there and began to farm the land.

⬣ *The Great Pyramids were tombs for the pharaohs of ancient Egypt. These three stone monuments still stand at Giza, near Cairo, the capital of Egypt.*

⬖ **The stone monument** *of the Great Sphinx has a man's head and a lion's body. It stands 66 feet (20 m) high, near the pyramids at Giza. The Sphinx was carved 4,500 years ago.*

Ancient Egypt was ruled by kings, called pharaohs. The Egyptians believed the spirit of their hawk god, Horus, entered a new pharaoh and made him a god too. They also believed in life after death. Pharaohs were mummified before being buried with things they wanted to take on to the next world. When a body was mummified, the dead person's internal organs (liver, lungs, stomach, and intestines) were removed and stored in special jars. Cats were also mummified when they died—they were sacred to the ancient Egyptians.

234

⬆ **Egyptian noblemen** *hunted in the marshes around the Nile. They used throwing sticks to bring down birds.*

◀ **It probably took 100,000 men** *more than 20 years to build the Great Pyramid. They used more than two million heavy blocks of stone. The pharaoh's burial chamber was deep inside the pyramid.*

⬇ **The wall paintings** *found in ancient tombs have told us a lot about the way ancient Egyptians lived.*

▶ **King Tutankhamun** *died at only 18 years old. He was buried in a tomb in the Valley of the Kings, near the ancient city of Thebes. This gold mask was found among the treasures in Tutankhamun's burial chamber.*

Ancient Greece

About 2,800 years ago, a new civilization began in Greece.

The ancient Greeks produced many fine buildings and cities. They wrote plays, studied music, and began a system of government that gave people a say in how their state was run.

Athens became the biggest and richest city-state in ancient Greece, with a well-trained army and a powerful navy.

Sparta controlled the

◆ **The Greeks** *were the first to build permanent stone theaters. In ancient times the actors were all men. They wore masks to show the sort of character they were playing.*

◆ **The Parthenon** *was a temple to the goddess Athene. Its ruins stand on the Acropolis—a rocky hill in Athens. The style of these columns is called Doric. A later, more decorated style was called Ionic.*

Ionic

236

Hermes　　Aphrodite　　Zeus　　Hera　　Demeter　　Hades

WHEN AND WHERE WERE
THE FIRST OLYMPIC GAMES?

The first Olympic Games were held in 776 BC in Olympia, a place dedicated to the god Zeus. The first athletes carried shields and wore helmets, but no clothes!

⬥ **Zeus** *was king of the Greek gods, and Hera was his wife. Hermes was the gods' messenger, Aphrodite was the goddess of love, Demeter was the goddess of grain, and Hades was the god of the dead.*

southern part of Greece. All true Spartans had to be warriors, and boys were trained to fight from the age of seven.

Rich Greek boys had their own slave. It was his job to look after the boy, take him to school, and help him with his homework!

DRAMATIC MASKS

PROJECT

Put a big plate on cardboard and draw around it. Then cut out the circle. Hold the cutout in front of your face and ask a friend carefully to mark the position of your eyes. Put the cutout down and cut out two eye holes to see through. Paint a happy or a sad face, and tape on a popsicle handle. Finally, stick on card ears and ribbon hair.

⬦ **Two kinds of Greek warship** *were biremes and triremes. A bireme had two banks of rowers on each side, and a trireme had three. Soldiers fought on the flat decks. The ships went very fast and were used to ram enemy ships.*

237

Ancient Rome

According to legend, the great city of Rome was founded by the twin brothers Romulus and Remus. The twins were abandoned as babies, found and fed milk by a female wolf, and later adopted by a shepherd.

From its origins as a village 2,700 years ago, Rome grew into a powerful city. The Romans conquered other peoples, first in Italy and then abroad. The Roman army created an empire that stretched around the Mediterranean Sea and reached as far as Britain. Roman soldiers built thousands of miles of straight roads throughout their empire. The cities had a constant supply of fresh water, carried to them along aqueducts from the hills.

◑ **Julius Caesar** *was a great Roman general in the last years before the first emperor. He was stabbed to death in 44 BC.*

◔ **The Colosseum** *was the largest amphitheater of ancient Rome. It could hold about 50,000 spectators.*

Centurions *were officers in the Roman army. Each one commanded about a hundred soldiers, who made up a century. The army was very well trained and extremely powerful.*

The Forum *in ancient Rome was an open public square. Citizens went there to discuss any important questions of the day together.*

The first emperor *of the Roman Empire was Augustus. He became emperor in 27 BC. This great leader set the style for later emperors.*

In AD 79, *Mount Vesuvius suddenly erupted and covered the nearby Italian town of Pompeii with volcanic ash. The town was buried and thousands of people were killed.*

The Middle Ages

Stained-glass windows *decorated medieval churches, and often showed stories from the Bible. The small pieces of colored glass were joined with strips of lead.*

The Middle Ages is the name given to roughly a thousand years of history, starting in about AD 500. This medieval period covers the history between ancient and modern times in Europe.

During the Middle Ages, European countries were ruled by a king or an emperor, who generally owned all the land. The land was divided among the

Knights *took part in tournaments, in which they fought against each other on horseback. One knight tried to knock another to the ground by hitting him with his lance.*

ruler's most important men, who were called nobles. The nobles were supported by knights, who were trained to fight. Peasants lived and worked on the nobles' and knights' land, growing food for both themselves and for their master.

⬡ **Kings and nobles** *built big stone castles to protect their lands. Castles were also homes. In the Great Hall of a castle, the lord, his lady, and their friends were entertained while they ate.*

⬡ **Printing** *had not yet been invented. Books were copied by hand by monks. They were often beautifully decorated in bright colors.*

⬡ **In medieval towns,** *people threw their trash into the streets, which had open drains running along them. Jugglers, actors, and other street performers entertained people in the busy markets.*

Languages of the World

Language is made up of the words we speak or write down. Words help us to communicate with each other, to tell each other things.

⬣ **The ancient Egyptians** *used a system of picture writing. Their symbols are called hieroglyphs.*

There are many different languages, and there are different alphabets for writing them down. People usually learn just one language as a baby, and one or two more when they are at school.

▶ **Here's how** *different people say hello. From the left, the languages are English, Chinese, Spanish, Hindi, and Polish.*

hello
ni hao
hola
namaste
czesc

⬣ **This chart shows** *the number of people who speak the world's major languages. Millions more people speak Chinese than English.*

⬣ **Native American peoples** *did not share the same spoken language, so they used hand signals to communicate with other Native Americans.*

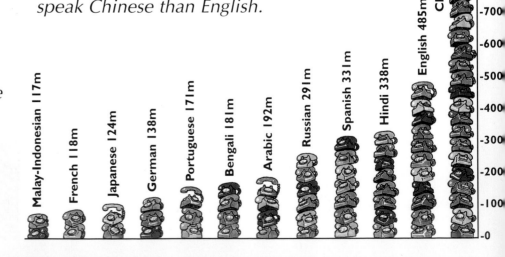

Malay-Indonesian 117m
French 118m
Japanese 124m
German 138m
Portuguese 171m
Bengali 181m
Arabic 192m
Russian 291m
Spanish 331m
Hindi 338m
English 485m
Chinese 1,300 m

АБВГДЕЖЗИ
ЙКЛМНОПР
СТУФХЦЧШ
ЩЪЫЬЭЮЯ

象 王 賊
是 是 奪
玉 玉 取
的 的 王

अ आ इ ई उ ऊ ऋ
ह ऐ ओ औ क ख
ग घ ङ च छ ज
झ ञ ट ठ ड ढ ण
त थ द ध न प फ
ब भ म य र ल व
श ष स ह

⬧ **The Russian alphabet** *has 33 letters, derived originally from the Greek alphabet. Russian is related to the Polish and Czech languages.*

⬧ **Written Chinese** *is made up of about 50,000 picture symbols. Each symbol, or character, stands for a word or part of a word.*

⬧ **Hindi** *is the main official language of India (there are 15 other important languages in India). Words are linked with a line across the top.*

⬖ **Arabic** *is the main language of many Arab nations in the Middle East and northern Africa. The Arabic alphabet has 28 symbols and is written from right to left.*

ساحة المهد

MANGER SQUARE

CAN FLAGS TALK?

Flags can certainly be used to send messages. In the international flag code, there is a different flag for all 26 letters of the English alphabet. Sailors sometimes still use flags to talk to other ships.

⬖ **Japanese writing** *developed from ancient Chinese characters. Japanese children learn to write gracefully with a brush and ink. Such writing is called calligraphy.*

Religions of the World

The world's main religions have existed for thousands of years. During this time, they have tried to explain the world and the meaning of life to their believers.

◆ **Jerusalem** *is a holy city for Muslims, the followers of Islam, as well as for Jews and Christians. The Dome of the Rock is sacred to Muslims as the spot from where Muhammad ascended to heaven.*

It is thought that over 75 percent of the world's people follow a religion. Religion has been a powerful force in shaping world history, and has inspired many fine buildings, paintings, and music.

♠ **The Sikh religion** *began in India more than 500 years ago. Sikh men wear a turban to keep their long, uncut hair in place. Sikhs follow the lessons of teachers called gurus.*

◆ **Buddhism** *is based on the teachings of an Indian prince who lived over 2,500 years ago. He gave up his riches and was known as the Buddha, or "Enlightened One."*

◑ **The River Ganges** *is sacred to Hindus. They bathe in it to wash away their sins.*

⬧ **Since Roman times,** *Jews have prayed at the Wailing Wall in Jerusalem, Israel. It is the last remaining part of the Temple of ancient Jerusalem.*

RELIGIOUS SYMBOLS

Siva, a Hindu god

A Japanese Shinto temple

A Buddhist statue

∧ Christian cross

A Jewish seven-branched candlestick, or menorah

The crescent moon of Islam

⬧ **A baptism** *is a way of welcoming a person into the Christian Church. Usually water is sprinkled on the person.*

Festivals and Customs

The world's most famous carnival *is held for four days every year in Rio de Janeiro, Brazil. There are street parades, costume parties, and dances.*

There are many different festivals all around the world. They usually celebrate a person or an event, and many of them happen once a year on special holidays.

Festivals are happy occasions, when people often dress up and dance. Like festivals, customs and traditions are handed down from one generation to the next. They are done the same way, year after year.

Santa Claus *traditionally brings presents to children at Christmas. He is based on Saint Nicholas, a real bishop who lived more than 1,600 years ago.*

PROJECT

Draw the shapes of a witch, a moon, a bat, an owl, and other ghostly things on colored paper and cut them out. Stick on decorations and glue the shapes onto a large piece of paper or cardboard. Sprinkle with glitter for a star-spangled Halloween finish, and put it up in your room.

◑ **At Halloween,** *October 31, children dress up in ghostly costumes, make jack-o-lanterns, and play trick-or-treat. It is a day for stories about ghosts, witches, and wizards.*

◑ **In Mexico,** *on the special Day of the Dead, people have a fun celebration in memory of friends who have died.*

IS THERE A DOLL FESTIVAL?

In Japan there are two doll festivals, one on March 3 for girls, and another on May 5 for boys. On these days children display the special dolls of their emperors and heroes that were handed down by their parents and grandparents.

◑ **Dragon dancers** *in the streets celebrate Chinese New Year. This is a time for family parties. The end of the New Year season is celebrated with a special Lantern Festival.*

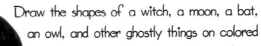

People and Places

Quiz

1. What is the name of the largest gorge in the world? (page 210)

2. Which is the largest state in the USA? (page 211)

3. What does the name of the Inuit people mean? (page 212)

4. In which year was the railroad across America completed? (page 213)

5. Which is the largest country in South America? (page 214)

6. How long is the Andes mountain range? (page 215)

7. What is the main language of South America? (page 216)

8. Who are gauchos? (page 217)

9. Which countries make up Scandinavia? (page 218)

10. In which European country could you find geysers? (page 218)

11. What is the name of a traditional Spanish dance? (page 220)

12. In which city can you see gondoliers? (page 221)

13. Which is the world's biggest continent? (page 222)

14. Why was the Great Wall of China built? (page 222)

15. Which country has more people than any other? (page 224)

16. What is the traditional form of Japanese wrestling called? (page 225)

17. Which two seas are joined by the Suez Canal? (page 226)

18. What is at the top of Mount Kilimanjaro? (page 226)

19. Where do scientists believe the earliest humans lived? (page 228)

20. What are "ships of the desert"? (page 229)

21. Where is the Great Barrier Reef? (page 230)

22. What are the three groups of Pacific Islands called? (page 231)

23. Who were the first Australians? (page 232)

24. What is the international date line? (page 233)

25. What were the pyramids used as? (page 234)

26. Which famous ancient Egyptian king died at the age of 18? (page 235)

27. Who was king of the ancient Greek gods? (page 237)

28. What did the first Olympic athletes wear? (page 237)

29. Who was the first Roman emperor? (page 239)

30. In which ancient city was the Forum? (page 239)

31. When were the Middle Ages? (page 240)

32. What weapons did knights carry in tournaments? (page 240)

33. What is the Spanish for "hello"? (page 242)

34. How many letters are there in the Russian alphabet? (page 243)

35. Where did the Buddha come from? (page 244)

36. Which river is sacred to Hindus? (page 244)

37. Where is the world's most famous carnival held? (page 246)

38. What date is Halloween? (page 247)

248

A

Aborigines The original people of Australia.
aerial/antenna Metal device to transmit TV and radio signals.
aerobics Exercises to keep you in shape.
algae Plants that grow in the sea, without true stems, leaves, or roots.
amphitheater Large stadium of ancient world.
antenna An insect's sensitive feelers.
aqueduct A narrow bridge carrying water.
astronomer A person who studies the stars, planets, and space.

B

bacteria Tiny micro-organisms, or germs.
brain The control center of the body.

C

carnivore An animal that eats meat.
cartilage Rubbery gristle that makes the skeleton of sharks and rays.
climate The weather conditions of an area.
cold-blooded With a blood temperature that varies with the temperature outside.
colony A large group of animals living together.
comet A snowball of ice and dust that travels around the Sun.
compass A device with a magnetic pointer that points north.
continent A huge land mass.
crater A round dent in a planet's surface.
crust The Earth's outer shell.

D

decibel A unit that is used to measure the loudness of sounds.
diameter The width of a circle or ball.
disk A small piece of plastic that stores computer information.

E

empire A large region under one ruler or government.
energy The ability to do work.
engineer An expert who plans, designs, and helps to build things.
equator An imaginary line around the middle of the Earth.
erupt To throw out rocks, gases, and other material.
evaporate To turn into a vapor or gas.
evolution The gradual development of life over millions of years.
extinct Not existing any more, having died out.

F

follicle Hole in the skin where a hair starts to grow.
fossil The remains of an animal or plant that are preserved in rock.
friction A rubbing force that holds up sliding forces.
fuel Stored energy used to power machines.

G

galaxy A very large group of stars.
generator A machine that makes electricity.
gravity A force that pulls everything toward it.

H

herbivore A vegetarian animal that eats only plants.
hoax A trick played to make others believe what's not true.

I

icecap A permanent covering of ice.
infectious Quickly spreading to others.

L

lance A long spear.
larva Melted rock that flows from a volcano.
Latin The language of the ancient Romans.
legend An old story handed down.
lens A curved piece of glass or plastic that bends rays of light.

Lent For Christians, a time of fasting leading up to Easter.
lever A bar that turns on a fixed point, to help us lift or force things open.

M

mammal A warm-blooded animal; baby mammals feed on mother's milk.
meteorite A rocklike object from space.
microscope An instrument that helps you see tiny details close up.
Middle Ages A period in history between AD 500 and 1500.
mineral A hard substance usually found in the ground in rock form.
mummy A dead body treated to prevent decay.

N

nectar Sweet substance from plants.
New World North and South America, described by exploring Europeans.
nomads People who wander from place to place to find food.
nutrient Something that nourishes the body and does it good.

O

oasis A place in the desert with water.
observatory A building with a telescope for looking at the stars.
orbit To travel around something.

P

pampas Flat grassy land of Argentina.
paralyze Make some living thing unable to move.
particle A very, very small piece of something.
plastic A human-made substance that can be molded into shape.
plate A piece of the Earth's crust.
pollen Powder made by male parts of a flower, containing male cells for making seeds.
pollution Damage caused

by waste and harmful substances.
Pope The leader of the Roman Catholic Church.
prehistoric Relating to ancient times before writing was invented.
prey An animal hunted by another for food.

R

range Series of mountains.
recycle To use waste materials again.
reef Underwater rocks.
robots machines programed to work in a similar way to humans.

S

signal A series of radio waves that can make up pictures and sounds.
state A country or part of a country.
stethoscope A doctor's instrument for listening to sounds.
streamlined Shaped smoothly for speed.

T

tentacle A long, bendy body part, like an arm.
tissue Groups of similar cells joined together to form parts of the body.
treaty An agreement between countries.
tropics Hot regions near the Equator.

U

umbilical cord The tube that feeds a baby food and oxygen while it is in its mother's womb.

V

vegetation Living plants and parts of plants.
vertebra One of the separate bones that make up the backbone.
vibrate To move very quickly back and forth.
vocal sac Folds of skin in male frogs that can fill with air to make a noise.

W

warm-blooded With a body temperature that always stays the same.
weld To join pieces of metal or plastic together.

Acknowledgments

The publishers wish to thank the following artists who have contributed to this book:

Julie Banyard, Martin Camm, Mike Foster (The Maltings Partnership), Ron Hayward, Gary Hincks, Richard Hook, Rob Jakeway Steve Kirk, Janos Marffy, Mel Pickering (Contour Publishing), Gillian Platt (Illustration Ltd.), Terry Riley, Mike Saunders, Guy Smith (Mainline Design), Roger Stewart, Michael Welply, Michael White (Temple Rogers), Michael Woods

All photos **Miles Kelly archives except:**
AKG Page 239 (TR);
Chris Bonington Library 24 (B)/Doug Scott;
Susanne Bull 86 (BR);
Corbis 172, 198 (T), 201 (T), 206 (TR);
E.T. Archive 242 (TL);
Honda Dream solar car 71 (B);
Gerard Kelly 85 (B);
Natural Science Photos 178 (T, BL), 186 (TR), 188 (TR), 191 (T), 201 (CL), 207 (C, TR);
Panos 229 (TR, CR);
PhotoDisc 10 (L), 11 (R), 20 (B), 22, 23 (B, TR), 26;
Rex Features 28, 29, 44-45 (B)/Greenpeace/Tim Baker, 46 (TR, BR), 47 (BL); 78-79 (C)/The Times/Simon Walker;
Sega Rally 77 (CR);
Science Photo Library 76 Geoff Tomkinson, 115 (R);
Patrick Spillane (Creative Vision) 100, 109 (CR), 115 (T);
The Stock Market 20 (C), 21 (TR), 35 (C), 42-43 (B), 47 (BR), 51 (TL, C, B), 51 (BR), 54 (C), 63 (B), 104 (TL), 111 (BR), 117 (T), 121 (C), 126 (TR), 232 (B), 233 (T), 244 (CL), 245 (BR);
Tony Stone Images 93 (TL).

All model photography by **Mike Perry at David Lipson Photography Ltd.**

Models in this series:
Lisa Anness, Sophie Clark, Alison Cobb, Edward Delaney, Elizabeth Fallas, Ryan French, Luke Gilder, Lauren May Headley, Christie Hooper, Caroline Kelly, Alice McGhee, Daniel Melling, Ryan Oyeyemi, Aaron Phipps, Eriko Sato, Jack Wallace.
Clothes for model photography supplied by:
Adams Children's Wear